Three

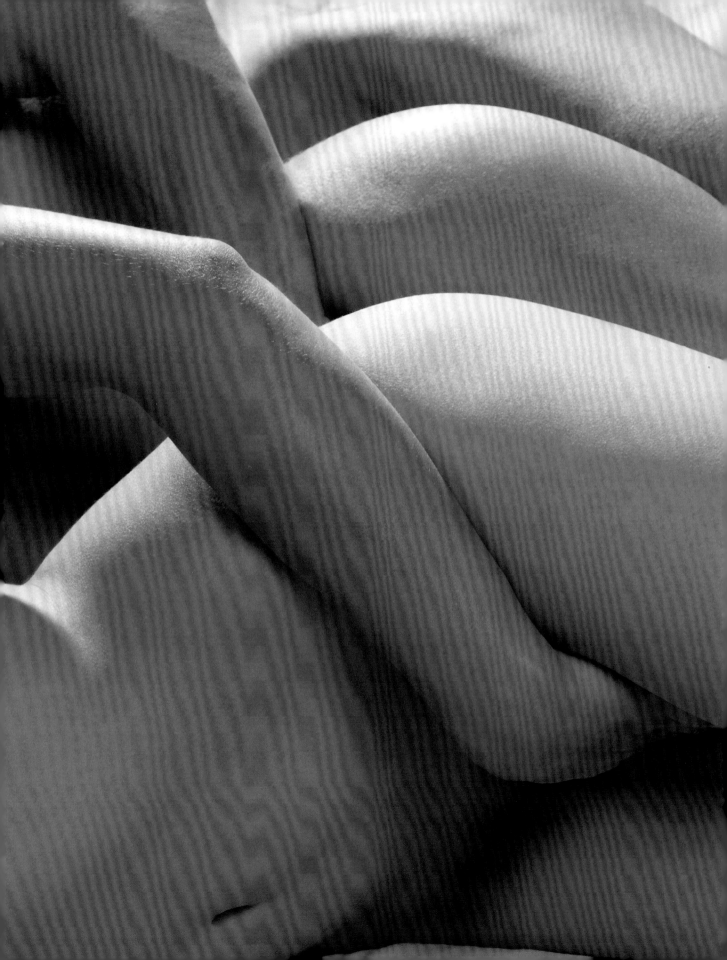

Three

THE ART OF THE MÉNAGE À TROIS

Sadie Johnson

STERLING/RAVENOUS

An imprint of Sterling Publishing Co., Inc.

New York / London

STERLING and the distinctive Sterling logo
are registered trademarks of
Sterling Publishing Co., Inc.

Library of Congress Cataloging-in-Publication Data Available
10 9 8 7 6 5 4 3 2 1

a ravenous book

Produced by Ravenous
An imprint of Hollan Publishing, Inc.
100 Cummings Center, Suite 125G
Beverly, MA 01915

© 2007 by Hollan Publishing, Inc.

Published by Sterling Publishing Co., Inc.
387 Park Avenue South, New York, NY 10016

Distributed in Canada by Sterling Publishing
c/o Canadian Manda Group, 165 Dufferin Street
Toronto, Ontario, Canada M6K 3H6

Distributed in the United Kingdom by GMC Distribution Services
Castle Place, 166 High Street,
Lewes, East Sussex, England BN71XU

Distributed in Australia by Capricorn Link (Australia) Pty. Ltd.
P.O. Box 704, Windsor, NSW 2756, Australia

The Producer maintains the records relating to images in
this book required by 18 USC 2257 which records are located at
Hollan Publishing, Inc., 100 Cummings Center, Suite 125G,
Beverly, MA 01915.

Printed in Singapore
All rights reserved

Sterling ISBN-13: 978-1-4027-4923-0
        ISBN-10: 1-4027-4923-6

For information about custom editions, special sales, premium
and corporate purchases, please contact Sterling Special Sales Department
at 800-805-5489 or specialsales@sterlingpub.com.

Cover and interior design by Lauren Vajda

To sexually curious explorers everywhere

Contents

Introduction

ménage à trois

The threesome is

the ultimate in sexual decadence, depicted in Hollywood and triple X movies alike as the holy grail of sex. While one can be fun and two certainly has its benefits, there's something about three that elevates the experience to mythic proportions. It's something that almost everyone wants to try. The thrill of two other bodies next to yours, the tangle of limbs, fingers and tongues, the threat of sensory overload. It's mind-blowing.

If this is the sort of activity you associate with freewheeling singles or couples whose bloom is gone, think again. In the world of sexual exploration, threesomes are on par with a mouth-watering meal at the chef's table in a fine restaurant—not something you'd do every day, but a fantastic, once-in-a-blue-moon moment no matter who you are or what your background.

I remember the first threesome I had wasn't technically a threesome at all. In fact, I sat on the sidelines for most of it, watching my lover go at it with a girl we'd met at a party. I felt like such a voyeur, sitting in the corner, playing with myself as I watched him with her. It was so incredibly hot that when she left, I attacked him. Of course, I made sure to participate the next time. —SARAH W., 32

THE HISTORY OF THREE

It's next to impossible to pinpoint when the threesome became a part of sexual culture. One could theorize that it's as old as sex itself. Some argue that the biblical relationship between Jacob, Rachel, and Leah constitutes a threesome. Depictions of threesomes show up in history as early as the Kama Sutra, the ancient Indian text on human sexual behaviors.

Though most commonly known as a threesome, the term also has aliases. The French refer to it as a *ménage à trois*, which literally translates to "household of three." This grouping is considered a relationship or domestic arrangement between a married couple and a lover in which some—but not necessarily all—participants are having sex.

Kinky trios aren't a thing of the past, and aren't just for the French. According to the 2005 *Durex Global Sex Survey*, 15% of people worldwide have engaged in a threesome. Australia has the highest percentage with 28% of Australians having participated in a threesome. Americans bring 24% to the table, coming in after Iceland, New Zealand, and South Africa. Who has the least amount of threesomes? India checks in with 4%. Looks like someone's not reading the Kama Sutra very regularly.

EVEN THE FAMOUS PARTAKE IN THREES

It's safe to say that if there's a trend, there's no way the rich and celebrated won't adopt it. Obviously the Hugh Hefners of the world have had more than their fair share of threesomes, but what's more interesting is the people you might not expect to be engaging in such activities. For example, take famous silent-screen star Greta Garbo. Though it was long rumored that Garbo was in fact a lesbian, the incredibly private and reclusive Hollywood legend was also thought to be bisexual, having had relationships with men and women throughout her life. Another famous experimenter in the world of three was Ernest Hemingway.

But if you're looking for more recent examples, you don't have to search for long before finding someone. You could bet the house on nearly any rock band from the 70s, 80s, and 90s engaging in threesomes, or look no further than admitted Heidi Fleiss client Charlie Sheen, who ordered up girls the way most people order Chinese food. Jean Claude Van Damme allegedly dabbled in more than one woman at a time. You'd be surprised how many Hollywood moguls and stars have participated in threesomes.

Because we're monogamous but still curious, my boyfriend and I have a game. We choose a famous third to make up a fictional threesome, then have a sexual encounter as if that person were there in the bedroom with us. Sometimes we play like they're just watching. Sometimes we use toys and pretend the toy is our third person. So, in the past three years I've had fictional threesomes with many of Hollywood's elite, like Cameron Diaz, Brad Pitt, Julianne Moore, and Robert Redford. I'd have to say my favorite was Scarlett Johansson. Not only is she incredibly sexy, but there was something about that evening that my boyfriend and I "shared" her, so to speak, that will forever be burned in my memory. —MINDY F., 29

Three ... In Film

Though not necessarily considered an Oscar contender, 1993's *Wild Things* wasn't without its artistic and erotic merit. The set-up for the plot plays out like one excruciatingly long tease, specifically highlighted by Denise Richards's wet and sexy car wash scene. But it's the scene in which Richards, Matt Dillon, and Neve Campbell engage in a brief but memorable tryst in a seedy motel room that leaves a lasting impression. While Dillon is sandwiched between Campbell's bad girl persona and Richards's good-but-dirty femme fatale in a Catholic school skirt, the three of them undress one another and share passionate kisses amid sips of champagne. It's a wonder this flick got by with an R rating!

FROM THEN TO NOW

Believe it or not, there was a time when threesomes were considered the ultimate taboo. Even though free love was a big theme throughout the 60s, it was thought that only a certain kind of person experimented with swinging—usually those who were into the whole hippie-love music scene. The 70s certainly upped the debauchery level, but even then it was thought to be strictly for the truly decadent partiers. As the 80s rolled around they brought a new consciousness and openness to discussing sexuality. The more people shared their fears, interests, and desires, the more the subject of threesomes entered the dialogue.

Now, threesomes are as American as apple pie, a solid part of our pop-culture vernacular. Threesomes have been part of storylines in TV shows like *Sex in the City* and *Seinfeld*, and movies have made them the plot as well as an interesting side story. More and more books discuss the "hows" and "whys" of threesomes, and erotic fiction describes in delicious detail some of the ways three can connect. The more three has gotten the spotlight, the more people want to know about it so they can try it.

WHY THREE?

One is nice when it comes to sex, but obviously two is better. Going for four can make things a little crowded and by the time you skate past five, you're in performer territory—you might as well be on stage at the Met. But three is a comfortable little number that pushes you just outside of your comfort zone without drifting too far into unfamiliar territory. Sticking to three can make that tangle of limbs a little easier to navigate, not to mention the body politics. With a trio you're less likely to alienate someone in the midst of your sexual experimentation. The smaller your group, the more focused your intent.

If this is your first attempt at sexual experimentation as a couple, three is a much better way to start than jumping into group sex, especially when your third is someone you both know, love, and respect. You have greater comfort and control to slow down, back up, or even accelerate! Three can start you on a path to bigger and better sex as you learn about yourself and your partner. It can be your ultimate fantasy come true, leaving you with the self-satisfaction of attaining your sexual pinnacle.

An Expert Opinion:

Author and spiritual cowgirl Sera Beak on "the power of the number three"

There's no denying the lure of a threesome, but did you know that part of that lure goes beyond the desire to have your sexual cake and eat it too? Sera Beak, author of The Red Book, *helps shed some light on what makes three such an alluring number in the bedroom.*

> Three's got some powerful mojo … Spiritually speaking, three is never defined as an "extra wheel," it's seen as sacred and divine and complete.
>
> —SERA BEAK, AUTHOR

What is the historical significance of the number three?

Three's been *around*, baby. The number three has a rich history dating back to ancient Babylon. Its symbolism and imagery can be found embedded within almost every culture of the world—Celtic, Greek, Indian, and even Tibetan to name just a few—not to mention in fairy tales (three little pigs, the three bears, et al.). One of the most sacred symbols within Christianity is, of course, the Trinity, representing the Father, Son, and Holy Spirit. God is often thought of as having three qualities: omnipresence, omnipotence, and omniscience. The number three was sacred to the Hebrews, as it represented the three key relationships: a human's relationship with him/herself, a human's relationship with the world, and a human's relationship with God. Three was also considered to represent the "signature of life" in God for many Hebrews. Across the spiritual blackboard, three traditionally signifies "completion" of some sort, "entirety," something holy, and even divine perfection.

What else is significant about the number three on a spiritual level?

It represents body, mind, spirit; past, present, and future; heaven, hell, and earth, just to name a few more famous triads. Many occult beliefs suggest a third way of being—between what is seen and unseen, what is known and unknown, and what is morally right and wrong. (Keep *that* one in mind as you're exploring what our "moral" society often considers a taboo sexual act.) If we check out the more Western forms of numerology (some that you may even find fluttering in the back of *Cosmo* and *Elle*), three represents creativity and self-expression—perfect for the bedroom!

Is there more sexual power in three versus two?

Yes. It's a result of the two getting together that *allows* for a third, but it's this third that brings the one, two, and three into one unified powerhouse of spiritual oomph—a sexy triple threat to the status quo. And if there's one thing the gods and goddesses like more than watching us humans take showers and pay taxes, it's watching us explore and break our own traditions and creatively express all our physical possibilities. To them, when we do such things, we're just simply and delightfully expressing our divine natures in human heat.

Bottom line: Three's got some powerful mojo. Spiritually speaking, three is never defined as an "extra wheel," it's seen as sacred and divine and complete. Getting down and dirty three-way just might be another key to heaven.

WHO MAKES TWO INTO THREE?

Two of the most common misconceptions about the act of threesomes is they're a last-minute, pull-out-the-stops, "Hail Mary" attempt to save a failing relationship, or that only kinky swingers from the 60s are into the sexual acrobatics that can become a threesome. But to approach such a delicious sexual experience with such a closed mind would be a mistake.

Who makes up a threesome is entirely up to your imagination and beyond. Sometimes it's the person you'd most expect to do it, like that sex kitten waitress at your favorite dive bar. Sometimes it's the people you'd least expect, like your parents! Not that you'd want to know about that, necessarily, but the point is to keep an open mind so you can keep your options open. Nothing can ruin the possibilities of a threesome faster than a closed mind, especially when you have preconceived notions about the kinds of people who like sexual experimentation. The first key to having a threesome is to be open to the possibility that almost *anyone* could be interested in having one. You never know until you try.

I'd had threesomes before, but they were never really something that blew my mind. Fun, sure, but I'd never shared one with someone I had a real connection with. Most of my girlfriends were against playing outside of the two of us, so when I met Sandy I assumed she'd be the same way. One night she and I were out at a club and we'd been drinking a little. I was shocked when she started flirting with a girl we both found attractive! She actually asked permission to take her home with us, and I could barely disguise how excited I was to hear her say that—it was almost more exciting than the threesome itself, which was amazing. Sandy taught me you can't judge a book by its cover. **—RICK M., 34**

EXPAND YOUR SEXUAL REPERTOIRE

Having a threesome isn't just another notch on your belt; it's a pretty unique one. Just as you learn from every singular partner you go to bed with, you can also learn from your threesome. Adding a third partner to the mix can help you out of a sexual rut, open you up to new experiences and sensations, and give you the opportunity to learn not only how a new body responds to touch, but how your body responds to different strokes. You might learn a new technique from your third that you can use on your significant other when it's just the two of you. You might also learn that you like the feel of something done to you in the heat of the moment that you can teach your main lover to resurrect at a later date. Old dogs *can* learn new tricks, especially when they're dirty!

One of the most important experiences you can draw from a threesome is a deeper connection to your sexual being. While it's great to make sure everyone is enjoying the experience, in the end it has to be good for you, too! Making the right threesome connection will ground you and help you understand your likes and dislikes, your desires, and what you respond to and when. Whether you wind up "threesoming" on a regular basis, make it a "special occasion," or only try it once, the experience and memory of it is something that will last a lifetime. Make sure it resonates where it counts most, in your own pursuit of sexual growth.

THE CHALLENGE OF THREE

One thing is for sure: You almost need a pilot's license to navigate your way through an extra body when you're used to having just one at your disposal! Before you get to that point, there are many things to consider: discussing it with your partner, making a plan, finding the right person, figuring out how it happens, etc. It all sounds daunting, but, as they say, with great risks come great rewards.

While you don't want to overthink the experience to the extent that you lose the joyous spontaneity of sex, some basic guidelines and etiquette will help your threesome experience be as smooth as silk.

Being tangled up in three can take you to an erotic dimension beyond your wildest dreams.

I'd been dreaming about having a threesome for so long that I think I psyched myself out for it—I'd built it up so much in my head that I started to worry that nothing else was going to compare to what I'd envisioned. As such, my first attempt at a threesome was an uphill battle, almost like I had to move heaven and earth to make it happen. But when I let go and went about it more naturally, everything just clicked. I still discussed it with my partner and we still laid down ground rules and agreed who our third would be, but once I set my intention in motion and let everything take care of itself, it turned out better than I ever thought possible.

—LISA Q., 25

HOW DO I KNOW IF I'M READY?

If you've read this far that's definitely a sign. Ask yourself this: Is a threesome a fantasy you've had for a long time? Is it something you've played out in your dreams or on your own with fantastic results? Is it something you can envision yourself doing in real life? Do you feel like you're missing out on something by not having one, but you just don't know how to get the ball rolling? If you've answered "yes" to these questions, it sounds like you're ready to take the next step to turning your fantasy into a reality.

So, let's get started . . .

CHAPTER *One*

when two become three

Everyone has fantasies—

that's the easy part. Turning your fantasy into a reality can be tricky if you don't have the right tools. As much as threesomes are something to be open to and spontaneous about, a little preparation can go a long way. So how do you get started?

DISCUSS IT WITH
YOUR PARTNER

It probably goes without saying that you and your partner need to be on the same page about whether or not to add to your bedroom activities. The fastest way for you to see your fantasy sink like the *Titanic* is to assume your partner is up for anything. Make some time to have an honest heart-to-heart with your partner about what you'd like to do.

THE TIME AND PLACE

The perfect time to bring up the possibility of a threesome isn't likely to be after dinner with your parents or during a fight, and it certainly isn't appropriate to discuss at the grocery store (even if the two of you are checking cantaloupes for ripeness). Only you know your partner well enough to know what time and place best encourages open and honest discussion. Choose your venue wisely. Essentially, the possibilities can be boiled down to the two that follow. They both share something essential to the success of your intention: privacy.

In Bed

For some, the perfect opportunity arises (pardon the pun) in the heat of the moment. You can use it as sexy foreplay, or save it for when you're in the throes of postcoital bliss. All depends on whether you have the ability to focus on the topic at hand. The only catch to talking about threesomes during sex is that your partner could mistake your discussion point as just a playtime thing. If that's the case, you may want to broach the subject both inside and outside the bedroom.

Out of Bed

Be it over dinner or cuddling on the couch watching TV, just take a moment to tell your sweetheart that you have something you'd like to talk about. He or she will know this is something you're serious about and give you the time and attention you need to address the situation.

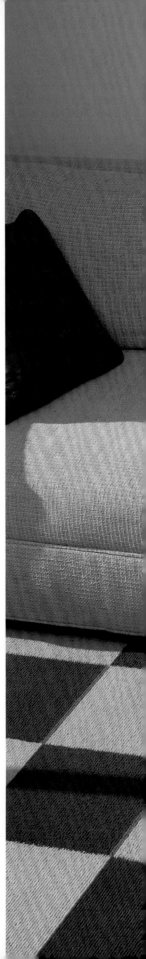

For some couples (but not all!), just fantasizing about the possibility of a threesome can get things hot between the two of you.

GAUGING THEIR REACTION

Your partner could have any number of reactions if you've never discussed this kind of activity before. What should you do in response?

Curiosity

If your partner reacts with more questions and comments but not an outright yes, don't take that as a bad thing. Curiosity toward a potential threesome is healthy, and means your lover considers it an option. This is not a time to be pushy. Answer any questions honestly; maybe suggest you two do some exploration and research together. Allow your partner the time to get comfortable with the idea and his or her feelings towards it or you might wind up with more solo time than you bargained for.

Anticipation

If your partner jumps up and down with glee and starts confessing threesome fantasies, you're golden. In fact, put down this book and get going! (Just kidding, of course. There are still tons of things you need to know.)

Ambivalence

If your partner doesn't seem to know one way or another how to feel about threesomes, don't fret. It doesn't mean the ship has sailed and your chances of having a threesome are as slim as winning the lottery. Accept your partner's reaction for the moment and go for a change of subject. He or she may just need some time to think about it, or perhaps is preoccupied by other things. Best to shelve the conversation for later and see if you get a different reaction.

Anger

If your partner blows up at you, the worst thing you can do is blow up back. The root of anger is fear, and your partner may just be expressing discomfort with an unfamiliar situation. The "don't push" rule applies here more than ever. Give your partner a chance to cool down, and when the dust clears ask honestly what it was about the concept that set him or her off. The key to a good sexual relationship is communication, so make sure that you're not the only one communicating openly, and you're welcoming the same from your partner.

Your partner may want to think things through before committing to a threesome.

Author and sexpert Rachel Kramer Bussel on "how to get someone interested in a threesome"

Though you don't necessarily want to coerce someone into doing something they don't want to do, sometimes all your partner needs to turn a "maybe" into a "yes" is a little encouragement. Rachel Kramer Bussel, author of many erotic anthologies and sex writer for Penthouse, shares her tips for getting your partner interested in some sexplorations.

Have you had any threesomes?

I've had several threesomes.

To you, what's the big deal about having them?

Part of it is that being with a third party is really exciting and you get to tap into that, more so than being with one person. There's less intensity, and not in a bad way, but with one person it's so intense that to have another person share that is sexy without pressure or awkwardness.

What are some common mistakes people make in trying to initiate a threesome?

I think guys have preconceived ideas of what a threesome is going to be like and get stuck on that—they don't let it unfold naturally. A guy forcing it too much makes girls skittish. I've heard of and seen girls enjoy making out or participating in threesomes that I wouldn't have expected to, mainly because it was completely spontaneous or it was initiated by another woman. The less you push someone to do something you want to do versus what would turn them on, the better. If the opportunity presents itself, a threesome might happen. You can't force the opportunity to arise.

So how do you bring it up to your partner?

I think it's good to float it by, if you're kind of like, "Have you ever thought of this?" I think some people talk about something and use it as a form of foreplay or talking dirty, and that's not a bad place to start. The fantasy can still serve you. One way to bring it up during a sexual moment when you're making out is you can say, "Angelina Jolie is hot!" and see if you can get some dialogue going. This may make it easier to bring it up for real. The bottom line is you just have to ask.

What if your partner is intimidated by the idea?

You have to find some part about the experience that would be sexy to them. Think about what they would want out of it as opposed to what you want out of it. I think a big thing people want is the reassurance that it's not about sleeping with someone else, it's about sharing an experience with them and watching them. In an ideal situation it's hot for everyone.

And if they're totally against the idea?

You can't push it. Either accept it or wait and see. Sometimes you have to let people think something's their idea. They might not say yes to you, but meeting the right third could inspire them to bring it up again. A lot of people are curious about it but wouldn't necessarily want to share their partner. I think you know if you're dating a person who would never want to do it.

> I think a big thing people want is the reassurance that it's not about sleeping with someone else, it's about sharing an experience with them and watching them. In an ideal situation it's hot for everyone.
>
> **—RACHEL KRAMER BUSSEL, AUTHOR**

When my husband first approached me about having a threesome, I was a little put off. Wasn't I enough for him? Wasn't he attracted to me anymore? So while initially I was concerned, he gave me some time and space to think about it on my own. When I was ready, I went back to him and talked to him about it. He told me that it wasn't that he didn't want me anymore, it was that he wanted us to try something new together. I was really grateful that he gave me the chance to mull it over on my own and then come back to him. It made me feel all the more secure about telling him yes when the time was right. —SUSIE M., 34

WHAT IF YOUR PARTNER DOESN'T WANT TO?

Of course, there is the very real possibility that your partner may not share your desire. If that's the case, you need to have a discussion with yourself about how determined you are to live your dream. Is it something your partner may warm up to later? Is there a creative way to work around it (see later on in this chapter for ideas)? If the answer to both these questions is no, you'll have to be happy with it remaining a fantasy or decide if this is something worth ending the relationship over. Obviously these are things only you can decide.

A threesome is about sharing with your partner, not excluding him or her.

FINDING YOUR THIRD

Once you've gotten the preliminary discussion out of the way, it's time to decide where to find the person who will turn your twosome into a threesome. This is quite possibly the second most important decision you'll make for your ménage à trois (the most important being the conclusion that you want to have one), as it will help set the tone for the entire experience.

GENDER

The choice you make regarding whether you'll add another woman or man to your mix will decide the dynamic for the evening. It can determine if you're going to be the focal point of the action, or if someone else is. Naturally, this depends on both you and your partner's comfort level, so make sure you have a frank conversation with him or her about it.

Adding Another Male to the Mix

Obviously there are pros and cons to adding another male to the mix depending on your gender and your comfort level. As a male, are you comfortable sharing both the spotlight and your girl with another man? Are you secure enough in your sexuality that, even if you don't swing that way, it's not going to freak you out if certain things get touched or brushed during the course of play? As a female, do you feel comfortable navigating two male bodies? Is that part of your fantasy, too, or would it be more for your partner's benefit? It's time to have an honest discussion with yourself to determine whether another man is the right choice.

Adding Another Female to the Mix

The same thing goes for adding another female. Guys, ego and bravado aside, do you really feel prepared to handle the desires of two women at once? How will you feel if the two women seem to do quite well taking care of themselves and each other: alienated or in heaven? For the ladies, is there any performance anxiety for you in terms of adding another woman to the mix? Does the thought of adding another woman turn you on or make you feel jealous? Really take the time to analyze the feelings that come up at the thought of another woman joining you.

When my girlfriend and I were making the decision of who we wanted to bring into our threesome fantasy-cum-reality, we sat down and discussed all the pros and cons of having another man versus having another woman before we even decided who that person would be. I was honest with her about my discomfort over having another man in the situation with us, and she confessed that she'd be more comfortable with it being another woman, so that made our decision a lot easier. It made our first threesome so successful that when we tried a second, I found a comfort level with having another man there so she could experience what I did with two females! —ROSS C., 37

WHO WILL IT BE?

Gender aside, figuring out who the right person is and where to find him or her is complicated. Thanks to the miracle of modern technology, your circle of friends, and your networking abilities, the option might be right under your nose.

FRIENDS

With friends, you already have a rapport and some kind of emotional connection. When all is said and done, this can either make things really comfortable or really awkward. Before approaching people within your circle of friends, make sure you have a handle on how adding that person could affect all involved.

How to Approach a Friend

If it's someone you know really well, approach it the same way you would if discussing it with your partner. Choose a private place and a quiet time to have a good, honest talk. Whether or not you want to include your partner in the conversation depends on your partner's closeness with said friend, and whether or not the friend would feel ganged up on if approached by both of you. Remember, the idea is to invite them, not creep them out. And don't feel awkward if they choose to pass. You never know if someone's going to say yes or no until you ask.

PICK-UPS

Sometimes the most exhilarating sex is with someone you meet out on the town and never hear from again. Of course, rules of safety do apply, but this can be one of the simplest options when choosing your third, if for no other reason than the stranger-in-the-night aspect.

Tips for Pick-ups

If you're thinking a good opening line might be, "Hey, are you up for a threesome?" you're wrong. Unfortunately there's not a step-by-step route to picking up a third. You're going to have to rely on instinct and keep the situation light. Start out with friendly conversation. Take the time out to get to know your person of interest. Then try a little flirting before graduating to more daring discussion. It's all about the subtleties, so if you need a little liquid courage to take the edge off, don't drink so much that you don't know which end is up. At the end of the night you can make a move and invite them back to your abode. If you've played your cards right, chances are they'll go with you. What happens from there is up to you.

One of my early threesomes was with a couple I met through friends of friends at a sex party they hosted. At the very end everyone left and I was there with the host and girlfriend, so it was kind of a foregone conclusion that I was going to stay. The guy took charge—he had been more flirty with me. It was very natural. We were just all in bed and they'd make out and then I'd make out with him and her. It was almost like when you're having sex with some person and it sort of moves from one thing to another, no awkwardness of who's going to do what, where does this go, it just happened. We didn't have to discuss every step. That's why I like threesomes with a couple, because they're doing it together, and with them it was sexy.

—RACHEL KRAMER BUSSEL, AUTHOR

Whether your threesome is with people you already know, or with people you've just met, it can be a very bonding experience if the right chemistry is there.

Three ... In Film

Though threesomes have been written about throughout literary history, none is more famous than the tale of Henry Miller, his wife June, and their lover Anaïs Nin. As the story goes, Henry moved to Paris and met writer Anaïs Nin, starting a wild love affair that wound up becoming a part of her well-published diaries. Meanwhile, June (thought to be bisexual) also became the object of Anaïs's obsession, though how far their relationship went depends on who you ask. Though Anaïs wrote about a sexual dream she had about June, many believe Anaïs's bisexualism was just a rumor. Regardless, the tryst was the inspiration behind the 1990 movie *Henry & June*, directed by Phillip Kaufman and starring Fred Ward, Maria de Mederios, and Uma Thurman. If that's not a hot threesome, we don't know what is.

ONLINE DATERS

Trying an online dating service gives you the best of both worlds. You can screen the person and get to know him or her, but also have the newness of a stranger to your advantage. An additional bonus: You can make your intentions clear in your online ad and cut through all the riffraff. While it may not be foolproof every time, the process of sifting through applicants is at least half the fun.

Making a Good Online Ad

Here's the one place you don't have to worry about subtleties and tiptoeing. With an online ad, it's best to put your intention out there. Explain in specific detail what you're looking to achieve, and with whom you're looking to achieve it. Do you have a preference for body type, hair colors, single versus those who are attached and swing? Now's the time to voice your desires and make quick work of finding your third. If efficiency is key, post something in the casual encounters section of a good online dating company.

SEX PARTIES AND SWING CLUBS

The more open society has become about our sexual interests and comfort levels, the more we've found places to express and explore them. Though sex clubs and parties have existed for as long as threesomes, it's much easier to find them now. Finding the one that's right for you might require a little research. Some are membership-only but often have nights for newbies. Many only require an entry fee, and some even have theme nights. Check out your options before you pick one, and maybe even visit a few before you execute your plan.

Creating Your Sex Party or Swing Club Tryst

Much like an online ad, one good thing about a sex party is everyone is there for action of some kind. That doesn't mean the basic rules of sexual etiquette don't apply. As a general rule, if a door is open and people are getting it on in the room inside, joiners are welcome. If the door is closed, obviously you're not to go in. Propositioning a third is much easier in this environment, but turning down or being turned down can sometimes provide temptation to take it too personally. When in doubt, check with the club for the rules of etiquette and play.

My boyfriend and I decided to use an online dating site to find the person we wanted in our threesome. We took our time crafting the ad so we could be super clear about what we wanted, as well as about who we were. We were overwhelmed with the response! It took time to go through the applicants, but we found the perfect person and had such a great time with her that we did it again! —JEN J., 30

STARTING FROM SCRATCH

Though most of the time we think of a threesome as initiated by a couple who seeks a third, that doesn't mean you can't have a threesome if you're single. In fact, it might be easier for an individual to navigate, considering you don't have to convince a lover or wade through discussions about monogamy versus swinging.

The same rules apply when you're hunting out your second and third, whether they're single or even a couple with whom to share the experience. When approaching friends, make sure you're gentle in your approach so no one feels awkward. Pick-ups might be harder to navigate, unless you happen to have a four-leaf clover in your underpants. Online ads are as simple for one looking for two as they are for two looking for a third. Sex clubs can also work for the single person. It's all a question of what you're comfortable with.

POTENTIAL PITFALLS OF THREE

Common issues that arise from threesomes include jealousy, anxiety, fear, and inhibition. But with a little tact and patience all of these issues can be addressed, easing your as well as your partner's nerves.

JEALOUSY

Often, jealousy arises from insecurity, for example, the insecurity that something will happen during the threesome to make your partner want the other person more. The key here is to assure your partner that it won't happen, and that the whole point of the threesome is for you to share and cherish the experience together. When your partner comes to understand that it's as much about them as it is about you, his or her fears will subside. If it helps, you might want to have a code word or a special touch that the two of you will share to remind each other that you're at the forefront of the other's mind.

ANXIETY

Once you've gone through the initial steps of making things happen, it's not uncommon to feel a little anxious about how the event will play out, and even about your performance. Relax! The more you obsess over every little detail, the more you're going to psych yourself out! The best way to beat anxiety is to be in the moment. If you're in the process of picking someone, enjoy that, and don't think a moment past it. Staying in the here and now will help you stay grounded for the there and then.

INHIBITIONS

Sometimes your inner sex god or goddess has a hard time coming out to play, and a lot of that has to do with mental blocks. If you're concerned about how you look naked, wear something that makes you feel sexy. If you think you look silly making an orgasm face, don't —you're not alone! None of us is perfect, least of all in bed. Allow yourself to enjoy the pleasure you seek. After all, two people who want to have sex with you are waiting, and you can bet they're not scrutinizing every inch of you.

FEARS

Sometimes, the closer you get to your fantasy becoming a reality, the more scared you become. It seems easier to have the fantasy than to live it. Just remember fears present us with an opportunity for growth unlike any other emotion. If it winds up not being all you'd dreamed, nothing says you have to do it again. But if it does . . . well, you know.

CREATIVE WAYS TO THREE

Traditionally, a threesome is thought of as being three people who engage in sexual intercourse. To limit the experience as such could exclude you from some other exciting options. Also, it may reassure ambivalent partners to know there are other ways to have a threesome:

- **The Voyeur**
  In this scenario, one person watches the other two have sex. Couples engaging in a threesome still have the thrill of a third in the room, but the sanctity of their coupling remains intact.

- **The Helper**
  A little more hands-on than the Voyeur, the Helper is there to assist with tongues and hands as needed, but doesn't necessarily get the blunt end of the stick, if you catch our drift.

- **Making Out**
  Who says all threesomes have to be naked affairs? Sometimes, a good round of kissing and heavy petting is all that's needed to fulfill a fantasy.

- **A Three-Ring Circus**
  Imagine you, your partner, and a third masturbating in front of one another while you tease and tantalize each other with sexy tales. Delectable!

The Pros of a Singlehood Threesome

- Not having to have a "where is this relationship going" talk.

- Convincing two other singles to have sex makes for less baggage all around.

- If you're the third with a couple, you are free to leave at the end of the night.

- You can afford to be a little selfish with your sexual needs. After all, it's expected!

- You can do what you want, when you want without worrying about trampling on your partner's feelings.

- Guilt-free threesoming!

Once my girlfriend and I had an agreement on our rules—she was allowed to do everything with our third, I was allowed to do everything but have sex with our third, and we were going to do it at our place. I almost couldn't wait for it to happen. When the time finally came, I was like a kid at Christmas! But having the rules in place beforehand made for a much better experience for all of us because we all respected them and each other. —MITCH J., 32

An Expert Opinion:

Porn Legend Nina Hartley on "why threesomes are my favorite things"

A lot of people wonder why threesomes are so great, especially when they've never had one. Porn legend and registered nurse Nina Hartley has had many and can talk first-hand about this great sexual experience.

How many threesomes have you had?

Hundreds. I have to leave it at hundreds. That number includes both professional and private threesomes, but I've definitely had hundreds of professional threesomes. I like them on camera so much because I like them at home so much.

So why do you enjoy them so much?

First, as a bisexual person, a girl/girl/boy threesome satisfies my personal taste of having one of each. I like men's sexuality and their parts, and I like women's sexuality and their parts. In a threesome scenario I get to have a smorgasbord. As a person who likes to help facilitate pleasure, I love assisting a couple in having a good time. Then, of course, there's the sheer porno thrill of live sex—watching it right there in front of you, where you can see, touch, hear, smell, and taste it. It's intimate, these two other people sharing a side of themselves that no one really gets to see.

But aren't threesomes complicated with couples?

Certainly it can be, but the ability to have an open relationship is an incredible thing. There's a difference between approaching the line and stepping over it. When you approach the line, you fantasize together, watch movies together, and discuss what's hot to both of you but you don't do it. To step over that line requires a sexual orientation and ability to be more open. A lot of people don't have that. The fantasy is common, but the ability to healthily do it, not so. You're either into multipartner sex or you're not. Just remember, threesomes are magnifiers. They can bring the negative as well as the positive of a relationship to light. They're nothing to be trifled with—the consequences are serious.

Is there any way to talk your partner into having a threesome?

I strongly discourage talking someone into something. Using force or coercion will result a bad experience for everyone; manipulation should be forbidden in a relationship. You have to talk about how intensely you want a threesome, and gauge that with the degree of resistance to it. If it's that important to you but your partner says absolutely, 100% no, you may have to break up and find someone who will do this. All vetoes carry equal weight, but depending on the reason for saying no, it's possible that over time, with good communication and trust, some interest in the idea might surface.

What are the best parts about having a threesome?

It is hot, sexy, and fun to witness and facilitate pleasure. Of course, the experience of a threesome varies depending on the specific dynamic and your role in it. There are three combinations that begin a threesome: as one of three buddies who share no emotional attachment; as a member of a primary couple with a third party; as the third party with a couple. How I behave with the other two and what I get from the experience depends on that specific triangle.

> Just bear in mind, threesomes are magnifiers. They can bring the negative as well as the positive of your relationship to light. They're nothing to be trifled with— the consequences are serious.
>
> **—NINA HARTLEY, PORN LEGEND**

Three . . . In Film

In 2003, Bernardo Bertolucci adapted Gilbert Adair's novel *The Holy Innocents* for the big screen. Called *The Dreamers* and starring Michael Pitt, Eva Green, and Louis Garrell, the movie follows Pitt's character of a young American exchange student who has moved to Paris and has a chance encounter with fraternal twins played by Green and Garrell. As their friendship grows, Pitt learns of their unusual bond and finds himself falling in love with the two of them. Though it's rumored that much more explicit sex scenes were planned for the film, both Pitt and Garrell insist that no such scenes were filmed (much to our chagrin). Both Jake Gyllenhaal and Leonardo DiCaprio were approached for Pitt's role, but Gyllenhaal passed due to the graphic nature of some of the scenes, while DiCaprio was committed to another role. Too bad! Regardless, the result is an intriguing and haunting tale sure to become an erotic classic.

SETTING THE GROUND RULES

Once you've had the talk, found your third, and decided what kind of threesome you're after, it's time to lay the groundwork.

WHERE TO HAVE IT

It could be that you or your partner feels more comfortable having your threesome at home, or at your third's place. And even then, maybe you want to keep it in the living room because the bedroom is sacred. Of course, there's always the option of going all-out and getting a hotel room. No matter what the choice, it's A-okay to dictate where the festivities will go down.

WHO'S ALLOWED TO DO WHAT

As with creative threesoming discussed earlier, it's perfectly fine to dictate that each person in the triangle is restricted to certain activities. Or, state that there are no restrictions at all. Just make sure you're on the same page. Even then, come up with some kind of hint to use if you get in the heat of the moment and want to take things in a direction other than previously discussed. Be prepared that it may or may not come to pass!

HAVING AN OUT

If someone isn't enjoying him or herself, you should all have the option to call an end to any activities, no matter how embroiled the others are in it. This will instill trust in all involved, paving the way for a retry in the future.

SPENDING THE NIGHT

We'll discuss this subject in chapter five, but for some people spending the night is far more intimate than sharing a sexual act. Make sure everyone knows where everyone else stands on this issue, and who's sleeping where.

Is the anticipation killing you? Don't fret. We're ready to move on to the next step: putting your plan into action.

Three . . . In Television

Seinfeld definitely made a name for itself with some of its more provocative episodes. Who can forget the bet, or the girl whose name rhymed with clitoris, or the girl Jerry dated who liked doing odd things in the nude? It's only natural that the gang would find a way to work threesomes into the mix. In one episode, Jerry decided that he'd rather date his girlfriend's roommate. What's a guy to do? If "take advice from George" jumped to mind, you're either a huge fan of the show, or not a very good decision maker. Yes, George steps up to the plate and encourages Jerry to suggest a threesome, thinking the girlfriend will get so offended that she'll break up with him, giving Jerry a clear shot at the roommate. Of course, the opposite happens—the girls agree to it, and Jerry backs out. You'd think everyone would learn their lesson from this one, but you'd be wrong. In a later episode, George attempts the same tactic in an effort to end his relationship by suggesting a threesome with his soon-to-be ex-girlfriend and her male roommate, until the male roommate agrees to it. So while we didn't actually see any threesome action take place, just the discussion of it was incredibly racy for network television at the time, and enough to get our imaginations going.

starting with three

After you've done the talking, the scoping, and the picking of your third, and the three of you are sitting in the same room together, there's a moment where it hits you: You're really about to have sex with two other people! How did this happen? What do you do? Whose idea was this, anyway?

Relax! It's human nature to go through a little bit of panic when one of your biggest fantasies is about to come true. That said, panic too much and you're going to send the whole thing south—and not in a good way. It can be a little intimidating to move from conversation to naked Twister, but that doesn't mean it can't be done!

GETTING THE BALL ROLLING

With all that anticipation coursing through your veins, it can sometimes be a daunting task to figure out your plan of attack, so to speak. It's best to take things slowly leading up to the action. Give yourselves time to find your comfort zone, and don't be shy about having some tricks up your sleeves to make sure everything runs smoothly.

SETTING A MEETING POINT

Unless your threesome knows each other well and doesn't have any performance anxiety, it's best to choose a meeting place that will give everyone an opportunity to sit down, chat, and get a feel for one another's vibes. You want to be able to ease into the night's activities. You might want to consider going out for dinner or to a local lounge or coffee shop. Wherever it is, it should be someplace where nobody feels pressured to leap into action, where you will have a chance to verbally feel each other out.

TALK A LITTLE, FLIRT A LITTLE

As everyone gets the chance to settle in and relax a little, it's perfectly reasonable for you to set your intention for the evening, but you'll want to do so subtly. In other words, don't blurt out, "So when you wanna do it?" Be suave, not pushy. Few things are as unattractive as

I think the anticipation was the worst part for me. I was just so nervous! I remember I was sitting there with my boyfriend and the girl we wanted to play with. There was music playing, soft lighting, and everything was in place for us to feel comfortable, but we all just sat there stone faced, completely incapable of looking at one another, let alone saying anything. After what felt like hours of ignoring one another, I looked at our third, she looked at me, we looked at my boyfriend, and all of us started laughing. We realized we were being silly, but it's hard not to be nervous—especially when it's your first time! —MARIANNE K., 26

someone trying to steer the conversation in a lascivious direction when nobody else is in that aspect of the game. However, that doesn't mean you can't throw in a few well-timed coy comments with a wink or a gentle nudge. A little flirting never hurts anyone.

TRANSITIONING

Chances are, after an hour or two everyone will be ready to take the next step. You'll instinctively know when this time has come; it usually involves more relaxed conversation and body language. When in doubt, simply ask if everyone is ready for a change of venue. Again, don't rush this, no matter how impatient you are. Be sensitive to everyone else's needs while taking care of your own.

LOCATION, LOCATION, LOCATION

Considering you've talked enough with your sweeties to have gotten this far, it's likely you've predetermined where the magic is going to happen. Whether it be a hotel room, their place, or your place, make sure you know your route and have plans on how to get there. For example, if you've met at a lounge and had a couple of drinks, make sure you take a cab to be on the safe side. If it's a lovely morning, afternoon, or evening, take advantage of the weather and the opportunity for more time to get comfortable and walk to the destination of your ultimate sexual fantasy.

STARTING IN NEUTRAL TERRITORY

Unless you're going at it en route, don't insist everyone head to the bedroom right away! Doing so prematurely will make you seem pushy and desperate, and you don't want that. Everything should happen naturally. It's best to continue the tone that was set at your meeting place, and congregate somewhere neutral like the living room—especially if the three of you are at your place or at your third's place. This will give everyone the chance to get comfortable with the surroundings and feel secure with the situation.

Three … In Television

Nip/Tuck has been known to push more than one button at a time throughout the course of their series—after all, the show deals with the ugly side of plastic surgery. But it's the studly Dr. Christian Troy who enacts many of our sexual fantasies, with threesomes coming out at the top of the list. In the first season, Christian cemented his Casanova status by bedding down with a set of young twins. Then there's the mother-daughter team he hooked up with in celebration of a milestone surgery. After picking the two up at a bar, the three retire to Christian's place where he takes his turns with both of them. Then there was the time Christian's girlfriend Kimber walked in on Christian and Kit, a detective in season three, getting it on. What else could she do but join in? Naturally that started a three-way relationship that lasted a long time. But all of those experiences paled in comparison to the tryst he shared with his business partner and friend Sean McNamara. Having lusted for Sean's wife Julia for years (an affair that resulted in a son that Sean thought was his) Christian and Sean resolve their differences over the situation by jointly seducing a Julia look-alike and sharing her for an evening of intense fun. Not to be outdone, Christian's son Matt has a threesome with a girl he likes and the girl she likes, until they get busted by their parents and get a stern talking-to. Way to ruin the mood, Mom and Dad!

SETTING A MOOD

Of course, you don't want harsh overhead lights calling attention to every pore on your face and the theme to *Spongebob Squarepants* blaring on the stereo, unless that's your particular kink. Think soft lighting, comfortable seating, anything to make your threesome feel cozy to the point where they might just want to get started right there! It's best all three sit on a level playing field, whether that means everyone is on chairs, a couch, or the floor. One of the keys to a successful threesome is ensuring everyone feels they have a say in the event. Take every opportunity you can to make everyone feel equal.

When my girlfriend and I decided we wanted to have a threesome, we got so wrapped up in the precursor details that it bordered on obsessive. She bought special candles, and I made sure our lighting was nice and mellow so nobody felt like they were in the spotlight. It was kind of funny, now that I think about it. But the good thing was, we all appreciated it. We'd strewn pillows all over the floor so we could all sit comfortably in a harem-like layout. It worked better than we thought it would. We never even made it to the bedroom! —DAN F., 30

THE JITTERS

It doesn't matter how much prep work you do leading up to the Big Moment, chances are you're going to have the jitters. Even though you might have had a bit of face-to-face time before you all strip down, it's perfectly reasonable to be a little out of sorts. Of course, there are a few things you can do to make this more manageable.

WHY HAVE THEM?

Have you thought about that? Really—ask yourself why you have the jitters. Are you worried you won't be able to perform? Do you have concerns about what's going to happen to you, your relationship, or your third after all is said and done? Identifying what is making you nervous will allow you to break it down. Demystify your fear and you will take the wind out of its sails.

Make sure your setting is right, and that everyone is on equal footing.

HOW TO COMBAT THEM

Just like when you're planning your threesome, it helps to have a plan to deal with the jitters when—not if!—they rear their ugly head. Here are some of the best ways to deal with pre-threesome performance anxiety.

Breathe

It seems so simple, and yet we tend to forget how to do it when we're in "crisis." When you're feeling anxious it's natural to hold your breath in an attempt to gain control over something. The irony is that doing so will actually feed your anxiety. Slow your racing heart and mind with a few really deep, breathing-down-to-your-toes breaths. You'll instantly feel calmer.

Take a Moment to Yourself

If deep breathing doesn't help, consider excusing yourself to have a little time alone. A few moments to sort out your thoughts can go a long way to resolving any residual threesome issues. Also, it can give you a chance to change your frame of mind. Think about another time when you were anxious at the outset of something and in the end everything worked out fine. See yourself in the situation, how you solved the problem, or how everything played out to your satisfaction. This can help restore your confidence. If the result of that greater feeling of control is that you decide to bow out of your trio, that's okay.

I had the jitters so bad that I thought I was going to throw up! There's something really scary about finally living out one of your biggest fantasies, you know? It's like you get so used to the wanting of it that the actual having of it becomes incredibly daunting. It took me a while to get over them. I'm sure my friend and my boyfriend thought it was never going to happen, but they were so good about making me relax that the evening wound up being the best thing that's ever happened to me sexually. —ANNEMARIE Q., 32

Don't let the jitters slow you down.

An Expert Opinion:

Writer and sex educator Jamye Waxman on "getting everyone ready for the experience"

Preparation is key when it comes to threesomes—not just for you, but for everyone involved. Jamye Waxman, a sex columnist for Playgirl *and* Steppin' Out *with a Masters in Sex Education from Widener University, tells how you, your significant other, and your third can transform a nerve-racking situation and get ready for what's to come.*

Have you had any threesomes?

Oh yes.

What was your first one like?

The first time I had one I was really nervous. It was me and a couple. They were excited and, while I was cool with the two girl/one guy scenario, it was still my first time. They sat on either side of me and didn't really touch me in a sexual way, but they held my hands and kept telling me, "This is gonna be fun!" It was all done affectionately so I didn't feel like they were going to jump my bones. I wasn't used to being with a woman. Her boyfriend left the room for a moment so she and I could talk, and she made a move while he was gone. It helped make it less overwhelming. We got intimate, and by the time he came back into the room, my fears were assuaged.

What are some of the things you recommend people do when they're jittery about their threesome?

Obviously one thing you could do to loosen up is to have a drink. Don't get drunk, but one social lubricant isn't a bad thing. It's an easy way to feel relaxed and get comfortable. Definitely start things off in a neutral space where you feel comfortable talking. If all these thoughts start racing around in your head and you're already in someone's bedroom, you might feel trapped. Go for dinner. If you wind up in someone's apartment, start out in the living room or some other safe space.

What do you suggest people talk about leading up to the event?

If you still have butterflies, it's okay to talk about that. Getting your fear off your chest will help you let it go. Talking is also good way to prep each other for what's to come. Be clear about what you like and don't like. You don't want to voice it like a list of demands; make it conversational, or even sexy and fun. If you don't like your butt played with, tell everyone your butt's off limits. It will make you less nervous and will help them get to know you sexually. While you're talking, warm up by focusing on what you find attractive in your partners. Feel free to tell them what it is, and soon you'll all be ready!

Are there any mistakes you can make in this stage?

Yes—thinking too much. Don't think too much once you've committed to being there; just *be there.* Also, you don't want to accidentally pair up. The key to a good threesome is to play fair and make sure nobody feels left out. Sit in a circle as opposed to a line. That will help everyone feel equal. In starting, keep everyone involved. Your focus should always be on one person; someone is kissing his or her face, the other is going down. While you're doing this, everyone stays connected to everyone else with a hand on a thigh or an encouraging look so nobody feels isolated.

What if there's someone who is still really anxious about everything?

This is one instance where making it seem like a twosome for a moment isn't a bad idea. If one person leaves the room, another can ease and arouse the anxious third. Or, decide that the two more relaxed people will focus on the nervous person. Tell him or her how hot they are, that this is going to be fun, that you're excited. Thank them for the opportunity. This is their choice, too. Last but not least, being affectionate and showing endearment that isn't sex-related can go a long way.

EASING TENSION

Believe it or not, even the most confident threesome participants feel a little anxiety now and then. A reassuring touch can make a world of difference. Offer a friendly pat on the leg to your paramour, or encourage a hug from your third. Something so simple can make a world of difference to you and yours, which will make the next steps so much easier to mount.

KEEPING THE TONE LIGHT

There's going to be a lot of sexual tension in the air. Maintain a delicate balance, conversationally speaking. Certainly keep a sexual tone going, but have fun with it. The more you enjoy yourself, the more others will too.

One of the things we did before our threesome was share war stories, particularly from high school. In a way it was kind of funny because, of course, nobody ever knows what they're doing in bed at that age, which was kind of reminiscent of how we felt then and there. But at the same time, the discussion of sex kept everyone's mind on the task at hand. It worked like a charm. —CAMERON K., 35

THE QUESTION OF PROTECTION

As with any sexual activity, it's your duty to be 100% honest and up front with your threesome participants about your sexual history, especially if that history includes an STD. Raising the subject isn't easy, but it's necessary. It's also important to discuss what kind of protection you're going to use for your sexcapades. Everyone has preferences, and now's the time to discuss them.

I was completely open and honest about my STD with the couple I wanted to have a threesome with, even though it was really hard. Sometimes when you tell people they freak out even though you haven't even gotten close to getting naked. Fortunately, both of them were very knowledgeable and took precautions to ensure they'd remain safe throughout the experience. We've had a few more threesomes since then because we trust each other implicitly. —RICH R., 27

DISCUSSING STDS

The hardest part about a sexual encounter when you have an STD is telling your partners. The best approach is to be straightforward. Don't joke, nor should you make it sound like a life-threatening disease. Encourage questions so your partners can know about what you have and how it can impact them. If the three of you are mature enough to be able to have a threesome, you should be mature enough to handle an STD discussion.

If you're on the receiving end of this news, don't panic. In fact, be thankful that your partner has enough respect for everyone involved to be able to discuss this with you. And while having sex with someone that has had or does have an STD raises your risk, being smart and safe about how you engage makes all the difference. And if that means saving play time for later to make sure everyone is educated and understanding, so be it.

CHOOSING CONTRACEPTION

Never assume that contraception is going to be taken care of by someone else. It's best to travel with your own chosen brand of condoms. After all, nothing can ruin sexcapades faster than an ill-fitting condom.

If you're threesoming with people you know well, shopping for contraception together can be a fun way to kick the festivities into gear. Just imagine getting loads of goodies to try out over the course of the evening!

Discussing STDs or contraception can be uncomfortable, but once you get those issues out of the way, you're free to enjoy yourselves—to the fullest extent possible.

Three ... In Film

Y Tu Mama Tambien was released
in 2001 to critics' praise and a
warm reception at film fests. It
won Best Screenplay at the
Venice Film Festival, was a runner-
up for the National Society of Film
Critics Awards for Best Picture and
Best Director, and even nabbed a
nomination for Best Original
Screenplay at the 2002 Academy
Awards. All this came as a surprise
considering the sexual tones of
the film, not to mention its
complexity. When Julio (Gael
Garcia Bernal) and Tenoch's
(Diego Luna) girlfriends take off
for Europe, they set about
convincing Luisa (Maribel Verdu)
to join them on a beach on the
Oaxaca coast. Just one problem:
She's married. When she
discovers her husband has taken
another lover, she flees to join
the two boys on their adventure.
Luisa takes her turns with each
of them, suggesting the two of
them get together as well—a
recommendation that's met with
resistance until one night, after
the trio has a lengthy discussion
about sex and masturbation, the
three of them fall into bed
together. This trio scene provides
the climactic moment viewers
were waiting for from the moment
the movie began.

BREAKING THE ICE

So you've gotten into your comfort zones, you're relaxed and well fed,
and there's no excuse not to get things going—but how? It takes
someone daring to break the ice to start the threesome.

WHO STARTS THINGS?

There's no hard and fast rule that says any one person is best at
making things happen. This is one of those go-with-the-flow
moments where you'll have to judge your partners' reactions. If
you're too pushy, that's a turnoff. Of course, the easiest thing would
be for the others to start it with a little kissing and cuddling, but if
your partners turn out to be timid, the onus will be on you to get the
party started.

Your best bet is to start things slowly. If you were engaging in a little
flirty touching during the "Getting Comfortable" stage, you can step
things up by letting the flirty touching become a little more lingering,
a tad more insistent. Maybe friendly little kisses become a longer than
a peck on the lips, or the discussion a little more sexual in terms of
admiring your partners and imagining what you'd like to do with them.
If all else fails to ramp things up, you can always try a sexy game.

KEEPING THE PACE

When you're in the beginning stages of your threesome, whether
you're the instigator or not, it's a good idea to keep pace with the
other participants. That means not rushing ahead. For example, if
they're still in the kissing-and-petting mode and you're already
naked, they're going to feel pressured. On the flip side, if everyone is
rarin' to go and tearing each other's clothes off, sitting there in a
parka will likely slow things down. Encourage the evolution of the
evening with some subtle, well-timed moves. Hopefully and most
likely, you'll be fortunate enough to enjoy the snowball effect of three
people getting turned on at the same time.

TAKING THE LEAD

Let's say you're the adventurous type—or maybe you're just impatient. There's nothing wrong with taking the lead. Being the instigator can take the pressure off of your other threesome participants if they're a little apprehensive about what's going down. Just remember: It's not a race. As much as you want to meet your own needs, you're not the only one having this experience. The same rules apply: Take your time and make sure you pay attention to everyone involved. If you're in doubt about your desire to drive the action forward, ask your partners how they're feeling. Communication throughout the evening is essential, at least until you reach a point where you need no words at all.

Consider yourself lucky if your group trusts you enough to take the reins. Directing threesome traffic is a privilege, and not one to take lightly.

We were so nervous about what to do that it was becoming evident that none of us were going to do anything. So finally I came up with an idea: playing spin-the-bottle. There was something innocent enough about the suggestion that made everyone agree it would be fun, even though we all knew it would be the catalyst to get us playing. We used one of the bottles of wine we drank earlier in the evening and spun, and kissed each other, and before we knew it, we weren't using the bottle at all. —MICHAEL L., 33

MASSAGING

A great way to move things to the next level is to encourage a little more sensual touch in the form of group massages. Maybe you can administer them to your partners, or two of you can work on the third. You can start clothed and work your way down, or even just do each other's feet—whatever everyone is comfortable with. The great thing about massaging is that it can be a great tool for relaxing all participants; it gives you an opportunity to learn about how your partners like to be touched and where, and can be perfectly innocent or completely dirty depending on the people involved. Break out that baby oil!

Three … In Literature

British novelist Adam Thirlwell published the book *Politics* in 2003 with a twist on the typical threesome relationship. This one was about a father/daughter relationship that comes between the daughter's threesome with a male actor and a bisexual woman. The sexual undertones of the tale are titillating—there are incidences of anal sex and fuzzy pink hand cuffs … oh my! Thirlwell gets wrapped up in the psychological and social issues surrounding threesome relationships, discussing ethics, etiquette, and what eventually turns into a love triangle. It's not always the most uplifting story, but it's an interesting one nonetheless.

KISSING

It can be tricky to figure out how to navigate kissing your partners so everyone gets equal face time. As well, of course everyone has ideas about what makes a good kiss, and where.

Peck, Peck, Peck

Don't kiss these two people the way you'd kiss your grandmother hello, but do start off slow and sensual. Kiss eyes, ears, cheeks, necks, fingers. Let your lips do the walking with both of your partners, sometimes simultaneously. For example, bring each of their hands to your mouth at the same time so you can peck at both their fingers together. Maybe in turn they'll take their two sets of lips at the same time and together kiss your eyes, ears, cheeks, neck, fingers … Nice.

One After the Other

Start out by kissing one of your partners while the other one watches. Then kiss the watcher the same way. Doing this will also help you all see how everyone likes to kiss and be kissed.

All Together Now!

Once you've gone through your warm-up and everyone has had the opportunity to kiss one another, why not try a more advanced method and have everyone kiss all at once? Obviously you can't get the same suction action going that you can with a one-on-one, but going nose-to-nose with two other people and entwining tongues and lips is a great way to seal the deal, not to mention quite delicious.

SWEET ANTICIPATION

Finally, the moment of truth has come. You are about to feel the flesh of two other people under your fingertips! Once again, follow the pace that's being set by the others. If everyone is in a rush and flinging their clothes off, go for it! If the mood is more soft and sensual, relish in the agony of an easy pace. Unbutton a button here, slide a bra strap down there. Whenever you can, show your partners you're ready to move to the next level without necessarily going all the way.

EASING INTO THE MOMENT

You've spent a lot of mental energy getting everything ready for this moment. You had the discussion with your partner, found the right third person, gauged reactions, decided on a plan of attack. Surely your brain is exhausted at this point, which is good! Stop thinking, stop planning, and let it flow. Settle into the moment and enjoy where you're at—you've worked really hard to get here! Of course, that doesn't mean you should forget the rules discussed so you'll know the difference between overstepping boundaries and letting things happen. Chances are your partners will be as lost in the moment as you. Just settle back and enjoy!

Getting undressed was the hardest part for our threesome. It was like that was the final frontier before really getting in the thick of things. I think all of us built it up in our heads as The Moment. The interesting thing was I kind of started things by taking off my shirt, and then my girlfriend took off her skirt, and our third took off her belt … We went around and around like that, each of us taking something off as we kissed and petted one another, and before we knew it we were completely naked. —BRANDON H., 29

CHANGING VENUES

One thing to know about threesomes is there's no wrong place to have one. So if you started in the bedroom and that's working for you, great! And if you started in the living room and it seems that's working out for all involved, that's great too! But if you're someplace where you want more privacy or another room is just more comfortable to you, you have every right to suggest a change of venue. However, doing so can be tricky, especially when everyone is in the heat of the moment. Don't be a dictator and demand that everyone get up and go *right now*. Instead, start the process by getting up and luring the others behind you using kisses as a tool. Take their hands to gently lead them and, if all else fails, tease them with a hint that you're off to the bedroom for a little solo fun that they might want to watch and join in on.

Are you wondering what's next? Don't worry. The fun has just begun!

CHAPTER *Three*

three degrees hotter

The ice has officially

been broken. You, your lover, and your third are about to get to it. Now is not the time to freeze up! Though sometimes the best sexual encounters are spontaneous, a little bit of planning can make sure everyone is satisfied.

GET INTO THE GROOVE

By this point you've made the room transition or are so in the mood that you've dissolved into a mass of bodies on the living room floor. Whichever it is, now's the time to really turn up the heat!

UNDRESSING

Undressing a lover is the final frontier before the sexual escapades you're about to experience begin. While undressing one can be a feast for the eyes under the best of circumstances, undressing two doubles your pleasure and your fun!

The key to using this moment to its utmost is to take your time, especially if it's your first. Undressing your partner and your third gives you the chance to both see and feel their bodies in a new light, getting a sense for how their bodies look and how they mesh with yours. Conversely, watch their reactions to you and to each other.

A fun way to approach undressing is to take one article of clothing off at a time until you're completely naked. For example, you take off your partner's top, he or she takes off the third's pants, and so on. If you're more into playing the hands-off-till-the-last-minute game, each of you can undress in your own respective areas of the room until you're all completely naked. If that sounds like way too much trouble to think about and you're already getting it on, nothing gets the point across like the good old feverish rip-n'-tear. It's all up to you!

It felt like getting our threesome going took forever, but when the three of us finally got undressed and started kissing and caressing, it was the hottest thing I'd ever experienced. I think there's something so incredibly magical about adding that third body to the mix. It ups the intensity of a sexual experience to a level that's beyond description. The three of us laid in bed kissing, cuddling, and grinding on one another until we couldn't stand it anymore, and when we couldn't … Well, let's just say it was quite a ride.

—MONICA M., 23

FEELIN' AROUND

Now is when your fingers should do the walking. You don't want to get too wrapped up in your performance just yet! Just as undressing is an important part in setting the mood for your threesome, doing a little touch-n'-tickle can teach you a lot about what will make your partners happy.

Don't start with the type of feeling around you do with lips and tongue so much as fingertips and hands. Fingertips down napes of the neck, collarbones, arms, nipples, all of these areas should give you some indication of what makes your partners shiver. Involuntary moans, goose bumps, raised nipples, and the like are a hint that you're on the right path. Then, when it's time to really drive the point home, you'll know exactly which erogenous zones to target.

Also, sensual (as opposed to sexual) touch or stroking can put people at ease if getting naked was too much of a reality check. Take some time out to show whoever is stuck in "pause" how much you appreciate them and their body with some light, loving petting. Soon, they'll be ready to move on to the next step.

LIP SERVICE

Replace the gentle touch of your hand with a gentle kiss from your lips, and you're well on your way to erotic bliss. Lips are great for traveling bodies once everyone is settled into the moment. What better way to work your way down to …?

Three … In Film

Cabaret (1972): Loosely based on the 1966 Broadway musical, *Cabaret* was directed by Bob Fosse and starred Liza Minelli as Sally Bowles, Michael York as Brian Roberts, and Joel Grey as the Master of Ceremonies. Though not specifically about a threesome, the movie's script is decidedly more risqué than the play, featuring a three-way relationship between Sally, Brian, and Max, played by Helmut Greim. When Sally befriends Max, he takes both her and Brian to his country estate, where he proves to be shady in terms of his ultimate goal: Does he want to pursue Sally, or Brian? The lines get blurred even further when all three of them, drunk on wine, share a sensual and seductive dance together. Eventually it's revealed that not only did Max bed down with Sally, but Brian as well. Things wind up becoming incredibly complicated in the end, but for a brief moment, the three shared a sexy common bond that drives the plot forward unexpectedly, but wonderfully.

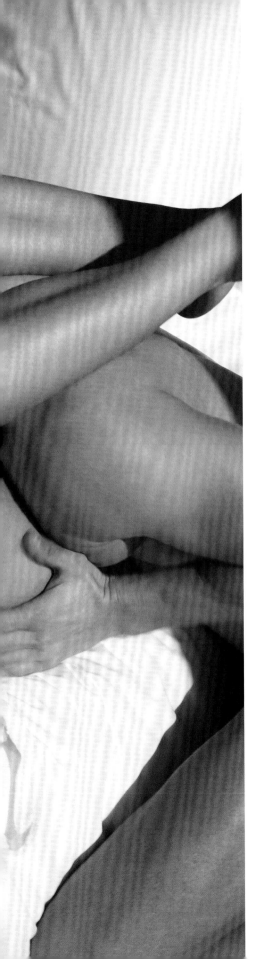

ORAL INCLINATIONS

Finally, we get to some sex! Not the main-course sex, but sex nonetheless. Obviously, how to have oral fun with one other partner is a breeze. But two? Things get slightly more complicated. That doesn't mean you don't have options. First, some pointers:

Going Down on Her

Chances are you've probably had some practice in this area; however if it's you and your partner sharing someone together, what works for your partner may not work for your third. If she's not the chatty type, remember to pay attention to nonverbal cues. Bucking hips, gripped bed sheets, and moans that wake the neighbors are all good things (unless you worry about being evicted). Stiffness, yawning, and involuntary twitching are not. Don't be afraid to ask for direction if you're unsure.

Going Down on Him

The same applies to ladies who happen to be in threesomes with two men. Just because your man likes a gentle scrotal tug doesn't mean your third will, too. The same rules apply. Look for nonverbal cues if he's not guiding you with words or his hands in your hair.

What Should the Third Do?

You might think that an activity like oral sex means one of you will be left in the cold, but you'd be wrong. Read on!

Take her cues when going down.

A Daisy Chain can be highly erotic.

Around the world ensures everyone gets a taste.

Two up top can be double the fun.

THE MAIN EVENT

POSITIONING THREE

Sometimes figuring out the best positions for incorporating everyone into your play can seem complicated. Don't worry. With a little creativity, you can make sure nobody is left out.

The Daisy Chain

Best as an oral position, the Daisy Chain can work in a number of ways depending on your threesome's gender makeup. For example, if you're two girls and a guy, the guy can lie on his back to receive fellatio from girl one, while girl two positions herself under girl one to give pleasure to the pleasure giver. The same scenario works well with three girls, three guys, and two guys with a girl. Remember to switch things up a little here and there so everyone gets a taste.

Around the World

A variation of the Daisy Chain, Around the World is exactly what you suspect it is. Everybody gets a taste. Instead of leaving one person's mouth unattended while another person's kit is left hanging, close up the circle so everyone's busy. You can all feel the love.

Two Up Top

This is best executed with two girls and a guy. As the guy is on his back, one girl rides cowgirl while the other sits on his face. The bonus is his hands are free to roam wherever he may choose, making for all the more fun for the girls riding shotgun.

Finger Cuffs

Named after Chinese finger trap toys, this position works well for those two guys and a girl scenarios. With the girl on all fours, one guy positions himself in front of her for some fellatio action, while the other enters her from behind. A word of caution: Finding a good rhythm in this position is essential if you don't want the girl in the middle to feel like a ping-pong ball!

This isn't strictly a boy/girl/boy position. Two girls and a boy can play this, too. For example, if one girl is in doggie-style with her man taking her from behind, the other girl can position herself in front of her for oral. Or, if the couple is going at it missionary-style, the third can straddle the girl's face.

Finger cuffs present a different kind of sexual puzzle.

The Sandwich

Best for two girls and a guy, you'll want to stack your partners like meat in a sandwich. For example, start with one girl on her back and invite the other to lie atop her face down. In this situation, your man meat will either have sex with the girl on the bottom, on the top, or both depending on how safe you are with one another.

The Cuddle

To the untrained eye, this position might look like it leaves one of your three unattended. Not so! If a girl and guy are having sex in missionary, the cuddler can snuggle in behind the girl on the bottom, offering more support, a warm body, and roaming hands into the mix. Conversely, she can sit behind a guy getting a cowgirl ride and let her fingers do the walking on either the guy or girl. The possibilities are endless!

The Triple Spoon

This one works well for almost any threesome combination. With a guy and two girls all laying on their sides facing the same way, the guy can curl in behind one of the women, entering her from that position, leaving his hands free to roam. While one girl enjoys the back-door action, she's free to curl her hands around and roam the front of the other girl to share the erotic entertainment she's getting. The same goes for the two guys and a girl scenario. This is one of those positions where everybody wins!

"Sandwiches" are yummy no matter the arrangement.

Cuddling during threesomes can be sexual, too.

Spooning provides some creative sexual options.

I loved taking time out to watch the action as it was going on! It added a whole other dimension to our play. The funny thing was, I was taking so much time out to sit and watch while I played with myself that my boyfriend and our partner kept coming over to me to pull me back into the action so they could enjoy me, too! That was probably one of the most memorable parts of our threesome experience. —JESSICA S., 29

THE BENEFIT TO "COLD" POSITIONS

Sometimes one person will wind up being the focal point, or sometimes you're just damn tired and need a break! In that case, don't feel bad about being on the sidelines. There are benefits to being the third wheel!

PLAYING VOYEUR

One of the hottest things you can do if you're not quite fitting into the puzzle is to become the voyeur. That might mean sitting on the edge of the bed to watch, taking a chair in the corner of the room, or even playing peeping tom, sneaking peeks through a crack in the door. Whatever your flavor, playing voyeur can be hot both for you and the two having sex, especially when they make eye contact with you! Best bet is they'll make it up to you.

BEING THE SOLOIST

You don't have to stop at being the watcher. Watching another couple have sex is like having a porn movie play out right in front of your very eyes. Take advantage of the moment and get your rocks off. When your partners in crime know that what they're doing turns you on, it will turn them on all the more. Plus, it's another way to show them how you like to be touched, and what gets you going. Whether you want to do it up close and personal by being right next to the action or have some distance between you and them is all a matter of personal preference.

How to Warm Up Your Threesome if You Feel Left Out in the Cold

- Be a worker bee. Make sure that lube is within reach, condoms are accessible, and water is replenished and waiting.

- Kiss, kiss, kiss everyone. Subtly but sensually inject yourself back into the action.

- Make the assist. Help whomever is the focal point of attention achieve one of many orgasms.

- Embrace the outskirts. Not all threesome activities have to include all three of you!

THE JOY OF UNPLANNED MOMENTS

You know everything you've been taught about setting the mood, positions to use, and whatnot? Forget it all. Just kidding!

It's always good to have a plan. Plans help set your intention, guide everyone in the right direction, and give everyone a common goal. They can also help you feel more secure about your activities with your lovers and friends. All the same, make sure you allow for the eroticism of surprise and spontaneity.

Though you might want things to go a certain way, clinging to expectations will almost definitely leave you disappointed. Be open to anything that might come your way. Maybe you'll try something you've never tried before, and like it! Or maybe you'll experience something you didn't enjoy. Either way, it's all a part of the process. The last thing you want to do is shut yourself down at the height of passion. Best to go with the flow, unless it's something that's really disagreeable to you. You never know what kind of journey you might go on if you don't give in and let go a little.

NAVIGATING LIMBS AND TONGUES

Admit it. If there's one thing that gives you pause when you fantasize about your threesome, it's how to work with an extra set of legs, arms, lips, and a tongue. After all, the thought of it is incredibly hot, and incredibly intimidating.

The key to working your way through a tangle of appendages is not to get too wrapped up in it, so to speak. If you think too much about what you're doing while the three of you are entangled, your head will overpower your loins and you'll lose the moment. Have fun with how wrapped up the three of you can get with one another, be it in a tangled embrace, or a tongue-twisting kiss. After all, if you wanted to stay on the safe side, you wouldn't be doing a threesome in the first place!

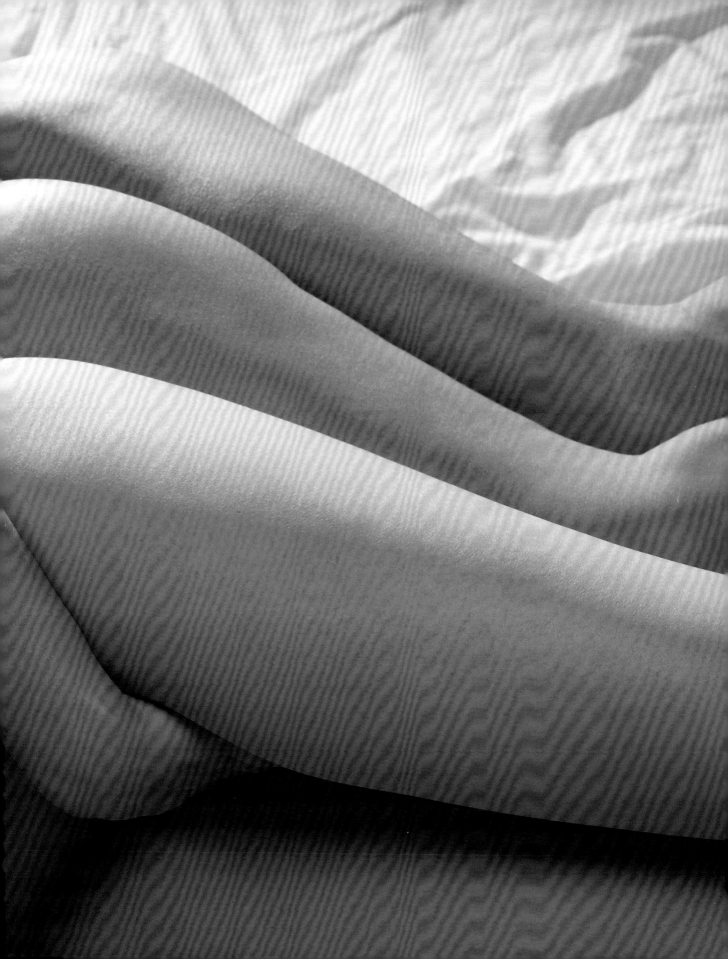

> At one point in our threesome, my boyfriend, our third, and I got so tangled up that it seemed like we'd gotten stuck, which was even better! We made it into a contest to see who could get the other off as much as possible working in such limited quarters. In the end we were trying not to get detangled because we were having so much fun! —KELLI S., 22

Three... In Literature

In the 1955 novel *Jules et Jim*, French novelist Henri-Pierre Roche tells the tale of two young men who are friends and the woman who loves them both. It was later turned into a film by Francois Truffaut in 1961 after Roche's death. In the movie, Jules (Oskar Werner) is a shy writer from Austria who makes friends with the more extroverted Jim. When the two of them meet Catherine she turns their world upside down. Though Catherine marries Jules, she has many affairs, seducing even their friend Jim. The result is an arrangement where the three live together until the story's tragic end. Most interesting about the tome is the rumor that it was based on the womanizing Roche's experience with Marcel Duchamp and Beatrice Wood, though that's not the only rumored inspiration for the story. Another threesome that Roche was supposedly embroiled in was with Franz and Helen Hesse—something Wood commented on in her autobiography, claiming the characters only bore a passing resemblance to the real-life inspirations. You know what they say: Write what you know.

SELFISH SHARING

It seems like these two words wouldn't go together, but pairing them actually makes perfect sense. This is the essence of how you should approach your threesome: with a yen for getting as much out of it as you can, while giving as much as you can give. As they say, you get out of life what you put into it. Threesomes are no exception.

TAKING CARE OF OTHERS

You have to be a giver as well as a getter if you want your threesome to go down in history. If someone is in need of a helping hand, give one. If a kiss will make someone feel good in the middle of an activity, do it. Ask if there's anything else you can do to help things go more smoothly, or help another achieve the pleasure they're looking for. Phrasing things in the form of a sexy proposition is a good way to ask for direction.

TAKING CARE OF YOURSELF

But by the same token, you have to be a getter as well as a giver! After all, this is your experience, too. Don't be afraid to speak up if your needs aren't being met, and don't be shy to show your partners what you want and need. If what you want isn't something they're comfortable giving you, see if there's an alternative. Take care of it yourself, if you can, or fantasize about what you want. Remember to be respectful of other people's boundaries and still enjoy yourself. You might just have to be a little more creative.

DEALING WITH WORST-CASE SCENARIOS

You might be lucky. Your first threesome might go off without a hitch, sending everyone through wave after wave of pleasure while meeting all your expectations and more. Or you might be unlucky. Everything that can go wrong will, leaving you to wonder if this was such a good idea after all. Of course, you could be right down the middle: nothing catastrophic, a few bumps here and there, a pretty good time had by all.

No matter which scenario you fall into, it always helps to have a plan ahead of time.

I think we were hypersensitive about worst-case scenarios with our threesome, which naturally meant everything that could go wrong, did. We banged heads and teeth more than once, the bed broke while we were on it, and as a grande finale, we knocked over a candle and set a blanket on fire. Luckily nobody was hurt, but still—It was like Murphy's Law had taken over! Luckily we had fun battling all the obstacles in our path and decided to try again another time. That one went off without a hitch. —MAXWELL P., 30

FREEZING UP

What happens if you're in the heat of the moment, but your body goes cold? It's not uncommon to experience a momentary flash of fear during the ultimate sexual experience—or not so momentary, as the case may be.

If this happens to you, remember the tools discussed earlier for dealing with the jitters? First, relax. Do a little deep breathing to get your body back in the action. If you still feel petrified, there's nothing wrong with taking a time-out and playing the voyeur role for a little while. If you can't bear not to be in on the action, there's nothing wrong with slowing things down to a level of play with which you feel comfortable. Backtracking to a little petting and cuddling might just be the antifreeze you need to get the home fires burning once again.

PERFORMANCE ANXIETY

Then there's the flip side of the coin—all systems are ready to go, except for one. The biggest mistake you can make in this scenario is to beat yourself up about it, followed by overanalyzing why it's happening. Do either of those two things (or both in tandem) and you'll be down for the count.

Instead, why not focus on giving someone else pleasure for a moment? Following that old adage about it being better to give than to receive can work wonders in situations like these. In the worst-case scenario, it just might not be your night, in which case, no reason to spoil anyone else's fun. In the best-case scenario, giving pleasure to someone else could re-rev your engines.

HUMOROUS MOMENTS

We've all had moments like this: You're in the throes of passion and one false roll takes you tumbling to the floor. Or, you're entwined in a somewhat air-catching position and someone passes gas. We're all human—it happens! Don't alienate your partners by being grossed out or accusatory. If it's you, don't be mortified. Best just to giggle about the mishap and move on.

In the case of falling off things, dropping things, spilling things, or what have you, go with it! Use it to your advantage. If the lube bottle explodes everywhere, get everyone all slippery and slimy and have some fun! If you all fall off the bed, maybe that's a sign you need more space and should take things to the floor! These are all instances where going with the flow can be to your benefit, and can make for some of the more memorable moments of your tryst.

JEALOUSY

Despite all the talking that you've done beforehand, there's no guarantee that either you or your partners won't experience jealousy. In the best-case scenario, it will be no more than a little tinge, just enough to make you cringe. In the worst case, this can lead to a massive blow-up.

Three ... In Television

It probably goes without saying that *Sex and the City* ruled the airwaves during its six-season run thanks in part to its frank discussion of all things sexual. In an early episode entitled "Three's a Crowd" Charlotte dates a man who wants a threesome, but she's not so sure about it. When she finally gives in, she discovers he's more interested in the other woman than her. Meanwhile, Carrie discovers Mr. Big was both married and had a threesome, information that sends her into a tizzy of insecurity. Samantha, the patron saint of threesomes, actually turns down the opportunity to have one with the man she's been seeing when she discovers he's married. Of course, she makes up for it in later episodes. When invited by a gay couple to be their first woman (an experience they want to share together), Samantha feels like the belle of the ball. Two gorgeous men ravish her body with kisses and compliments until they decide they can't go through with it and suggest going out for gelato instead. Later still, despite her insecurities about being an older woman, Samantha agrees to gift her boyfriend, hotelier Richard Wright, with a 21-year-old restaurant hostess. It all goes upside down when the girl calls him "daddy"—something that pleases Samantha greatly.

In the case of your partner getting jealous, you know him or her best. You can tell when a stiffening is from a forthcoming orgasm or from annoyance at what's going on. If it's the latter, make eye contact. Ease back from what you're doing. Use nonverbal cues to make sure your partner knows this is an experience that you're sharing with him or her. If that doesn't help, a time-out is in order. Naturally there's the chance that the action might not resume, but what's more important to you is that there be no a problem between you and your significant other. And if that means rescheduling your threesome for another time, so be it.

If you're the one feeling the pangs, take a moment to examine why. Is it because your needs aren't being met? If that's the case, are you speaking up enough about what you desire? Is it because you've suddenly had second thoughts? Whatever the case may be, a moment of reflection can help you determine the root of your issue, and whether or not it's something that needs to be addressed out loud, right then and there. If you do feel the need to speak up, don't be afraid; this is your threesome, too.

Now that you have the basics down pat, are you ready to turn up the heat? C'mon! Let's go!

One time in a foursome my boyfriend and I were having with another couple we were close friends with, the condom broke while my boyfriend was having sex with the other girl. The next day she had to get emergency contraception. He offered to go with her because he felt like he should be supportive, but her boyfriend wasn't thrilled about it. Things were okay between all of us afterwards, but it took a few weeks for things to even out. I'm glad that happened with friends. I think it would have been really awful if it had happened with a stranger.

—AUDACIA RAY, AUTHOR

Nothing in this world should be taken too seriously, and threesomes are no exception.

stepping three up

By now you're a

veritable expert on threesomes. You know
the hows, the whys, the best positions,
what to do with your tongue, and where.
You name it, you've done it. Chances are
you enjoyed your first experience so
much that you're going to want to do it
again, and again, and again. Why not try
something fun and different?

WHY STEP IT UP?

You're probably saying, "If it ain't broke, why fix it?" And you have a good point. But what if it's not fixing it? What if it's putting a supercharger on it, customizing the paint, and adding some ground effects? Okay, maybe that's a bad example. How about this one—a basic chocolate sundae is yummy, but sometimes it's fun to throw on some exotic nuts, extra whipped cream, and maybe some caramel sauce to mix in with the fudge, right? That's the same attitude you should be taking with your threesome.

I think we'd been doing the same thing over and over for months when my girlfriend approached me about switching things up. Initially I thought she wanted to have a different person as our third, which I wasn't really comfortable with. I thought we had a good thing going with the person we chose as our partner. But then she told me she was also happy with that person, and instead wanted to see what the three of us could explore together in making things feel a little more adventurous. I have to admit it piqued my curiosity . . . and that was enough to get me hard over the whole idea all over again. —DAVID G., 37

FAMILIARITY BREEDS CONTEMPT

If you've found people you like to pair up with and have established a comfort level with them, that's fantastic! You now have a surefire threesome whenever you want it. But do you want it the same way every time? Sure, there are variations on the basics, and it will never be exactly the same every time. But the more the three of you see each other, the more routine the sex will be. The reason you wanted a threesome in the first place was to try something new. Believe it or not, you can reach that "routine" moment within a threesome, too.

SPICING UP YOUR FAVORITE DISH

With a few simple adjustments you can take your threesome and make it a different experience every time—one that will be just as hot and memorable as the first time. These tips will make it feel like a new experience every time.

HOW TO STEP IT UP

There are a million ways you can make a threesome more original and exciting. The following suggestions are some of the most popular choices.

TOYS

Ahhh, such a simple thing can give so much pleasure. No matter what your comfort level with vibrators, dildos, and the like, there's something for everyone. A sex toy is an easy, non-intimidating addition to some already fun play, and it's almost guaranteed to increase your orgasms. Now, who wouldn't want that?

ROLE-PLAYING

Role-playing can be slightly more intimidating, but that's part of what makes it all the more fun. A little risk can be a great aphrodisiac! The types of roles you and your lovers want to take are only limited by your imagination. Let it run wild!

S&M

Not for the faint of heart! It's not recommended to jump right into the nipple clamps/candle wax/zippered hood type of stuff (talk about going from zero to 160!). Why not have a little fun working your way up? A tame, little tie-up-and-blindfold game may be just your thing.

DRESS-UP

Taking the role-playing or S&M scenario one step further, dressing up can really get you into character. Whether you're decked out in the finest lingerie you can get your hands on or a sexy French maid's outfit is up to you, but there's something about being someone else for a while that can make the fantasy go over in an incredible way.

LOCATION CHANGES

Who wants to stay in the bedroom all the time? What fun is that? Whether a change of location means changing rooms or changing actual venues, a new setting gives your senses a little jolt, which can help you feel fresh in the sack.

Three ... In film

It was bound to happen: an actual film about an actual threesome, not just in the sexual sense of the word, but the relationship as well. In *Threesome*, Lara Flynn Boyle plays Alex, a female college student who winds up sharing a dorm room with Stuart (Stephen Baldwin) and Eddy (Josh Charles) when the housing office thinks she's a guy because of her name. Though she's initially hesitant to stay in her living situation until administration deals with it, she settles into the groove and the three become friends, but not without complications. Eddy has a thing for Stuart, who has a thing for Alex, who has a thing for Eddy. The climax arrives when the three fall into bed with one another and share one passionate night. Even the hyper-hetero uber-jock Stuart gives in to Eddy's advances in the name of living in the moment. Though the movie was widely panned, it provides an incredibly hot moment in mainstream cinema.

While having a threesome is an adventure in itself, having one in a hotel room can make it even hotter.

QUICKIES VS. LONG, DRAWN-OUT AFFAIRS

Chances are your first threesome was some kind of Olympic event that ran overtime. And why not? If a blind man gained his sight, he'd want to walk around looking at everything as much as he possibly could! But just because the first time lasted forever doesn't mean a quickie can't be just as good.

We're only scratching the surface. Let's delve into these a little deeper and fully explore their possibilities. Before we do that, we need to take one of the most important steps: discussing it with our partners.

DISCUSSING WITH YOUR PARTNERS

Just like when you were in the throes of threesome fantasies becoming realities, you'll want to discuss with your partner and third whether or not you want to explore a new direction.

RAISING THE SUBJECT

Depending on how well you mesh with the other two people in your threesome, there's always the option of bringing up the subject while you're in bed. However, if one or both of them is touchy, this may feel like an ambush. Best to do it over dinner, drinks, or when you're all in a playful mood. This shouldn't be work. After all, you worked to make this threesome happen in the first place. Have fun with it, and see where the conversation goes.

GAUGE INTEREST

Do you remember the signals you were looking for when you broached the subject of a threesome with your significant other? You're going to want to look for those same cues again, except this time with both of them. Giggling, coy exchanges, and playful banter are all good signs; crossed arms, clamped-shut mouths, and cold body language are not. It could be the subject matter, or it could be the timing. Only you know for sure whether or not it's worth broaching the subject again later.

BE OPEN TO THEIR IDEAS

Seeing as your threesome isn't a dictatorship, be prepared—and excited!—to hear some of their ideas. Encourage open and honest communication, no matter how outlandish some ideas seem.

Some Great Sex Shops

- Hustler Hollywood (www.hustlerstores.com), with 12 locations spanning the United States

- Coco De Mer (www.coco-de-mer.co.uk) in Los Angeles

- Eros Boutique (www.erosboutique.com) in Boston

- Babeland (www.babeland.com) with stores in Los Angeles, Seattle, and New York

- Come As You Are (www.comeasyouare.com) in Toronto

- Good Vibrations (www.goodvibes.com) in San Francisco and Berkeley

- Womyn's Ware (www.womynsware.com) in Vancouver, Canada

- Venus Envy (www.venusenvy.ca) in Halifax and Ottawa, Canada

- JT's Stockroom (www.stockroom.com) in San Francisco

If you let your partners know you're interested in hearing what they have to say, you're creating an environment where you can also share your most creative self. Besides, you never know, you might be enticed to try something you'd never thought of before!

FIND A COMFORT LEVEL

If you're all in agreement that some extracurricular activities would be fun to add to your repertoire, work with your partners to paint a picture of what that might look like. Do new boundaries need to be set? Is there something that one person is okay with that another person isn't? Should there be a safety word? Now's the time to address such things so that when you're ready to go, there are no obstacles.

TOYS

Nothing can take a threesome to the next level as simply and quickly as a toy. Chances are you already have some at your disposal, but if not, adding one to your repertoire is as easy as pie.

WHERE TO BUY THEM

There are two avenues to take when shopping for sex toys: good, old-fashioned brick-and-mortar stores, and the Internet.

Brick-and-Mortar Stores

Most major metropolitan areas have some kind of sex shop somewhere. It all depends on how intrepid you are about your sex toy shopping. If you can find a high-end sex store that tends to cater to women, you don't run the risk of encountering the "ick factor" you find in the kinds of stores with the windows blacked out and men in raincoats inside.

Online Stores

If you'd rather remove the guesswork from deciding which brick-and-mortar store will offer what you're looking for, online stores might be right up your alley. The pro about ordering online is that it's easy and discreet (if you're the shy type), but the con is that you don't have the opportunity to see the toy, smell the toy, and feel the toy in action (with your hands—get your mind out of the gutter!).

WHO TO GO WITH

If you're up for the adventure of visiting a store in person—and good for you if you are!—obviously you have the option of either going it alone or taking your partner along. If you want to turn your outing into foreplay, why don't all three of you go together? Make your way through the store as you feast your eyes on the available products, teasing each other with possibilities and testing things out by hand. Just wait until you get home to try things out for real!

HOW TO BUY THEM

Simple. Got cash or a credit card? Then you're good to go. For some online stores you can use a PayPal account if you have one. Best to check their shopping and privacy policies if you worry about what payment method to use or what will happen to your shipping information when you enter it into their site.

WHAT TO GET

The possibilities are endless! If it's your first toy as a group, it's probably wise to stay on the relatively tame side and stick to something penis-shaped with a good vibration. However, if you're the more adventurous types, the sky is the limit! This is where going to the brick-and-mortar stores would be in your best interests. They often have samples of each toy in the store to poke and prod at your leisure. There's no better way to get a feel for what you want when you can actually *feel* what you want.

There are so many different types of sex toys available these days that you can even buy waterproof ones for bath or shower fun.

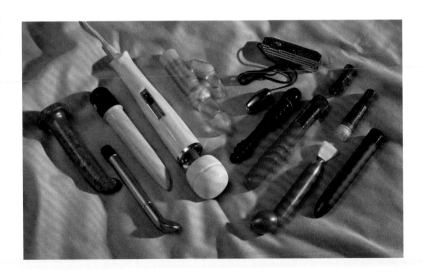

INCORPORATING THEM INTO PLAY

If you know a sex toy is something everyone will love and you don't need to worry about discussing it ahead of time, surprise your lovers by hiding it under a pillow or somewhere equally accessible so you can whip it out at a moment's notice. Otherwise, bring it to the festivities as if it were another partner, and give everyone the opportunity to be in control. You never know what might feel good where! Don't be afraid to speak up when something doesn't work for you.

SAFETY CONCERNS

As with any other sexual activity, you'll want to make sure your toy play is safe. That means no inserting it into one person right after the other, even if you all know each other really well and don't mind swapping spit. Going from one orifice to the other can introduce foreign bacteria and make for unpleasantness down the road. Best to cover your toys with condoms, removing and replacing them as you play from person to person. When you're finished playing for the day, make sure you clean the toy. Depending on what it is, you might want to ask for cleaning advice from the outlet from which you purchased it.

Sexy lifestyle expert Dana B. Myers on "why you should incorporate sex toys into your threesome"

To toy or not to toy? That is the question! Lifestyle expert and owner of BootyParlor.com Dana B. Myers offers her suggestions on how to steam up an already hot threesome with the inclusion of some playthings.

> Toys are great because they make a threesome more of what it should be— a fun experimentation, and help take some of the awkwardness out of it. —DANA B. MYERS, OWNER OF BOOTYPARLOR.COM

Have you had a threesome?

If you include inviting a battery-operated date into the bedroom, then yes, I've had a threesome.

Why would people want to incorporate toys into their threesomes?

Toys are great because they make a threesome more of what it should be—a fun experimentation, and help take some of the awkwardness out of it. Threesomes are the opposite of an intimate experience, by their very nature. You're not communing in a one-on-one way with another soul mate. You're exploring the limits of sexuality. You're playing. And toys underscore the "play" factor.

What can adding toys do for the experience?

In addition to lightening the mood, they can definitely heighten the experience. Let's face it. When there are three people, you can't always please everyone all of the time. Certain toys, like a double bullet vibrator for example, allow two people to be pleasured at once, while the third is either receiving pleasure from one of the participants or giving it. Strap-on dildos let two women be penetrated at once when there's only one male in the mix.

How should they go about introducing the idea to the other participants?

The easiest thing to do is ask! If the three people are already open to the idea of a threesome, chances are they will be ready for some toys. But if anyone balks, just remind them that it will make it easier for everyone to get pleasure continuously and will take some of the pressure off the partners, particularly the male in a two-girls-and-a-guy scenario.

What if someone is intimidated by the idea of including toys?

Toys shouldn't be intimidating, especially if you choose small, fun, buzzy toys. You don't need to introduce a 12-inch dildo. A small bullet, a couple's ring, or even a Rabbit should add a sense of fun and added pleasure—not anything threatening!

What toys do you recommend for threesomes?

We carry a lot of toys that are good for threesomes. Don't Stop Massage Oil is great for treating each other to massages. Perhaps one person could be sensually massaging another, while the massage recipient paints sexy words onto the third player with Melt Chocolate Body Fondue.

Dust Up is another fun body treat that trios can incorporate into their bedroom play. Dust it all over necks, breasts, legs, and have one person watch as the

I'd always wanted to bring toys along when we had our threesomes, but my boyfriend worried that it would presumptuous for me to do so, or that it would suggest that one or all of us were incapable of properly pleasuring one another, despite us all having had countless orgasms between us. So one night when we were having dinner before we went home to play, I raised the subject in a way that was playful, saying that I had a bag of tricks I wanted to use that night. That got both of them interested, and we spent the rest of our dinner talking about what we were going to do to one another with the goodies I'd brought along. By the time we made it to dessert we were practically all over each other. That night was so memorable; I still fantasize about it to this day! —MARISSA P., 28

other two lick it off each other. The third party will want to join in soon! The Twins are the best bullet for threesomes because this toy actually has two bullets that work in sync, as I mentioned. So if it's a guy and two girls, he can please both women at once with the same buzzing patterns on their c-spot, breasts, or anywhere he chooses.

The Turn Me On Vibrating Panties can be a lot of fun with three people. One lucky person wears the sexy panties with the vibrating bullet, another controls her orgasms with the remote control, and the third person can pay full attention to either of the other two, or just sit back, service themselves, and watch the fun! The Love Heart Harness can be a great addition to threesomes with two girls and a guy because it allows one of the women to wear it and use it on the other woman while she's penetrated by the guy. This is for adventurous threesome participants only!

Are there any toys that aren't good for threesomes?

There really aren't any specific toys that aren't good for threesomes. What works for two people will definitely work for three! Something to consider is the gender mix of the threesome. If you've got two guys and a girl and neither guy is gay, you probably won't need another phallic dildo. Beyond that, the sky's the limit, and it's really just up to the tastes of the participants. One suggestion is for the three people involved to shop for their toys together. You don't have to go to a store. You can shop online, and choose the toys that interest all three of you. Then, as the threesome date gets nearer, you'll have something to get even more excited about.

If you could have a threesome with or without toys, which would you pick and why?

I'd definitely choose to have a threesome with toys. I think the potential to have more pleasure and bigger orgasms is much higher.

ROLE-PLAYING

Do you remember how fun it was to pretend to be someone else when you were a kid? Maybe you had elegant tea parties and pretended to be queen of the castle, or you were slaying dragons, or you were your favorite rock star for a day. Whatever the scenario, everyone has done it at one point or another, though most of us drop the act as we grow older. But why? One of life's simple pleasures is stepping outside yourself to examine the possibilities of what else you can be, and that sentiment is no different in the bedroom.

The greatest thing about role-playing is that it gives you permission to be different than your regular sexual self. If you're normally a shy, retiring violet in bed (yes, even within the confines of your threesome), taking on a role-playing challenge can give you the opportunity to test out what it would be like to be a screaming banshee. Conversely, if you're always the loud one in bed, taking on an alternate persona might give you the opportunity to test out your strong, silent side. Though it's still authentically you having the experience, in a way it's not, which changes the playing field considerably.

DO YOU HAVE TO BE A GOOD ACTOR?

If you were auditioning for a role in a Hollywood movie, probably (though even then it's questionable). But this is your boudoir. Nobody is going to be hard on you if your English accent isn't up to par, nor are they going to kick you out if you don't really have a peg leg (if that's your role, of course!). This is something to have fun with, not obsess over. The key is to *believe in your role*. So if you believe in it and your partners believe in it, you're off to a good start.

HOW TO DO IT

The best way to get a role-playing scenario down is to create a short story, and to make sure that each of the players understands their part. If your story has something to do with someone being in charge, make sure the person playing that role is comfortable in a dominant scenario; likewise if there's a submissive role. That's not to say that you have to have a script down pat, but you should have a general idea of who is doing what and how the story will unfold to sex. Whether or not you decided to keep up the act during the sex part is up to you. Sometimes that's the most fun part of playing make-believe!

Role-playing can add a new dimension to your threesome.

IF YOU LOSE YOUR COOL

When you fall off a horse, get back on. The same thing goes for your role-playing. If you feel like you flubbed your role, you start to laugh. Or maybe something else throws you off your game like the phone ringing or an inopportune appearance by your favorite pet. Try not to let it derail you too much or else you might lose the moment.

IF THEY LOSE THEIR COOL

Likewise, if one of your partners falters in their role, you can help them recover by playing your part. You can say things in character to help them recover, maybe commenting on the situation that made them lose it. Anything you can do in character to help your partners stay on track will keep the role-playing fantasy alive.

IF ISSUES ARE UNEARTHED

Sometimes role playing games hit a little too close to home. If there's a role where someone is jealous, heavy dominance and submissive play, or maybe someone says something just the right or wrong way, it can trigger something for someone else. In those instances, it's best to stop play and address the situation right away. You can tell the difference between an instance when one of your partners simply needs to be coaxed back into character and when something said or done has touched a nerve. Use your instincts. If it's the latter, behave lovingly and tenderly as you resolve the situation. You can always role-play another day.

Some Good Role-playing Games for Threesomes ...

- The jealous husband (or wife) who comes home to find his spouse in bed with another person and then joins in on the fun.

- The hard-nosed boss who is seduced by two co-workers.

- The shy, quiet, virginal geek who is seduced by two stunning beauties.

- The rock star leading an extravagant lifestyle with a bevy of babes.

- The handyman who comes over to fix something, and finds a delicious surprise waiting for him.

- Three hot Hollywood stars pleasuring one another between scenes in their trailer.

- The vampire attacking helpless maidens, turning them into wanton sex goddesses of the night.

- Three random strangers in the night cross paths for a memorable tryst.

A little dominance never hurt anyone.

S & M

Ahh, a little dominance and submission, slave-and-master action. This is one of the easiest role-plays to take on without having to don an alternate persona that requires you to act. Though "sadomasochism" might seem scary, it's not as intimidating as it seems. All it means is one (or two) take more of a leading role, while one (or two) take a more passive role. You'll never know what you can discover about yourself sexually playing a role you're not used to taking in bed. The results can be surprisingly tantalizing.

IS IT GOING TO HURT?

That depends. Do you want it to? S&M doesn't have to be about paddling and whipping unless you want it to be. If you're unsure of what you'll think about it, start out slowly with just a blindfold. Allow yourself to be tied to the bed with scarves instead of handcuffs. Maybe try some playful spanking with an open hand. You can set your own limits and change them later. Start out slow, see what you like and don't like, and take it from there.

You should never feel inhibited about showing erotic pleasure during a threesome (or any sexual experience for that matter!).

TOOLS OF THE TRADE

You don't necessarily have to go out and buy a whole new wardrobe and supplies to add a little S&M into your threesome, but if that's what you want to do, go for it! Chances are you have something at your disposal to tie someone up and blindfold them, and if you're spanking with implements, a hunt through your house will turn up some useful tools. But if you're really a stickler for authenticity and want to go as far as dressing up for the role, try checking out fetish shops like Boston's Eros Boutique (www.erosboutique.com) or San Francisco's JT's Stockroom (www.stockroom.com). Both offer secure, discreet online ordering if you don't happen to live in those cities.

SAFETY WORDS

Before you begin your foray into S&M play, make sure you and whoever the submissive is (or submissives, if there are going to be more than one) have agreed on a safety word to alert the dominant player that the play is being taken too far. Most experts recommend you not use a word like "no," as that could potentially be considered part of the game. Aim for a word that has nothing to do with the activity. Maybe you like the idea of using "pizza" as your safety word, or a color like "yellow." Whatever it may be, make sure everyone is on the same page before you jump into your activity.

GETTING INTO IT

Once you get rolling in your S&M scenario, don't worry too much about how you look or sound. Lose yourself in the moment, just as you would in any other sexual experience. You're going to get the most out of play time if you're feeling with your body rather than thinking with your head. That said, if the feeling in your body is more of a painful pain rather than a hurts-so-good pain, speak up and use your safety word to set the boundary.

TESTING YOUR LIMITS

As you get more and more comfortable with S&M scenarios, you can create more of a challenge for yourself by testing your and your partner's limits. This not only requires an incredible amount of trust between you and your partners, but also builds trust. After all, if you're the dominant one, you're being entrusted with your submissive's well being, and if you're the submissive, you're

Three … In Film

Films seem to love threesomes, and *Three of Hearts* is no exception—though it is a bit more of an unorthodox approach to the event. William Baldwin pays a straight gigolo, Kelly Lynch plays his lesbian best friend, and Sharilyn Fenn plays Lynch's bisexual former lover. And if that's not convoluted enough, the three of them get involved. It all begins when Lynch enlists Baldwin's help in making Fenn believe that heterosexual relationships are inferior to that of lesbian pairings, until Baldwin and Fenn fall in love. Then, of course, Fenn discovers the ruse, which ruins the plan further. With lies, deceit, and sexual innuendo, *Three of Hearts* isn't the most heartwarming threesome tale committed to the silver screen, but the chemistry and attractiveness of the cast certainly helps make it one of the most seductive ones.

entrusting the dom with your well being. But no matter the role, don't be afraid to see what it's like to push things one step further. Don't do it all at once, but a gradual ramp-up of activities, sensations, and challenges can heighten the sexual experience for everyone involved. Once again, don't forget your safety word.

WHAT IF SOMEONE CRIES UNCLE?

The first thing you need to do is to stop immediately. As much as this is your good time, it's also both of your partners' good time. If it's more important to you to continue doing what you're doing despite one or both of your partners using the safety word, this kind of activity isn't for you. Stop the activity and take time out to converse with whoever called for the break. This will help build trust between the three of you, and show that you care for the people you're experiencing this with.

I remember one time my boyfriend and our third, a girl we met online and wound up having several threesomes with, tied me to the bed and blindfolded me. It was amazing because my senses were heightened. They'd run prickly things on my feet, or pinch me somewhere and follow up with tender kisses. It was torturous, but exquisitely so. When we finally started having sex—with me still tied up, mind you—I felt like I was having a full-body orgasm. It was amazing. —NANCI K., 31

DRESSING UP

You don't have to wait until Halloween to get dressed up! Just as with role-play or S&M, dressing up to fit the part makes the fantasy feel like reality. When you were five and slaying dragons, didn't it help to have a sword? The same principle is in play here. The more you can do to make your fantasy authentic, the more surreal and amazing the experience will be!

WHAT KIND OF OUTFITS?

How involved you want to get in dressing up for sex all depends on you—it can be as much or as little as you'd like it to be. For example, maybe your version of dressing up is a sexy lingerie outfit you picked up at Victoria's Secret. Or maybe you want to delve deep into a role-playing game and seek out that maid's outfit that makes it feel completely authentic.

You don't have to go out to a costume store to play dress up, unless that's part of your fun. Often the outfits you need are right in your own closet: a suit to play boss woman or boss man, flashy club-wearing gear to play rock star and groupies. For girls, the makeup aspect is always fun. Don't be afraid to experiment with looks and colors you might not always wear! After all, this isn't the everyday you, this is the fantasy you!

If you simply can't find anything to wear in your own home, there's always the option of going to a costuming place for just the right look. Some sex stores will have sexy costume versions of classic outfits, like doctor and nurse uniforms and schoolgirl outfits. Hunt through with your partner and your third to find the outfits you like, and then get excited for the coming attraction!

My girlfriend had this fantasy about having a hard-nosed boss crumble under her and a co-worker's feminine wiles. Our third had a home office, so we played out the scenario there, with me sitting at a desk in a suit and tie, and the two of them dressed in little skirts and high heels, with their hair tied back like sexy secretaries. They walked into my office and I started to lecture them, and at one point I turned my back to them as I was ranting. By the time I turned around again they were both standing there in nothing but their heels. My girlfriend crawled across the desk to kiss me while our third started undoing my pants, and suddenly I was over being such a mean boss. It worked out so well that we dressed up and played that scenario out more than once, though the next time my girlfriend was the hard-nosed boss! —JOHN Z., 28

An Expert Opinion:

Tech Girl and Sexpert Patricia Lee on "why dressing up and S&M makes a threesome that much more fun"

Transitioning from the sexual play you're used to into realms of role-playing and dominance/submission can seem intimidating, but if you let it overpower you, you're missing out on a fun new way to enrich your threesome. Patricia Lee, the tech girl and resident sexpert of ErosBoutique.com, offers some helpful hints for getting everyone on the same page with some new games to play.

Have you ever had a threesome?

Hell yes! Hasn't everyone? I remember the best part about my first threesome was finally finding out what it feels like for a guy when he caresses a woman's breast. Even better, I remember the second time, when I found out what it feels like to have two guys working on me at the same time! The neat thing about threesomes is the back and forth of it all. It's totally different when you are one of two women than when you are the girl with two men. I think everyone should try both.

What are some creative ways to take your threesome to the next level?

Personally, I think adding toys and temptations is a great way to bring a threesome to the next level. The best temptations I can think of are light bondage toys. Blindfolds and cuffs are probably the most erotic ways to bring on a new level of passion, and when you mix that in with a threesome it opens a hallway of new doors.

How do you recommend incorporating light S&M activities into your threesome?

It depends on how receptive the rest of your threesome is. If you've been screwing around a while with your playmates, then adding a little S&M is as easy as pulling the leather blindfold from your crotch where you had it cleverly hidden, grinning, and dragging it from a guy's nether regions slowly all the way up to his eyes. Follow closely with your tongue for extra effect! Once on, do as you please. Everything you do is now peaking past any sensation it previously produced. A touch can now be a tingle that fires right into the groin. It's all about the intensity of the unknown. From here, pulling out the whip is a given, don't you think?

What if someone is nervous about it?

I have a creative answer for that: fuzzy. If your playmates are nervous, bring on the fuzzy stuff. Fuzzy cuffs, fuzzy blindfold, even feather-ended teasers work wonders on intimidation. Colors like pink or purple, too—just make it cute, because that removes the sinister aspect that makes people nervous. Often if you also let the nervous person be the dominant one, it lets that person fantasize about having things done to them by practicing first. Tie the pink satin blindfolds onto yourself and throw your body down onto a lube-covered PVC sheet! No matter how nervous they are, they'll want to dig in!

What are some good role playing games for threesomes?

Hanzel and Gretel—oooh, that wicked whore witch taking advantage of those two innocents! Doctor, nurse, patient—oh my god, need I say more? Maid (or butler) of the manor—what's the penalty for missing a spot? Principal, teacher, and schoolgirl—better make that a naughty, *naughty* schoolgirl! Cops and robbers—or, more popular lately, cops and mobsters!

Do you recommend playing dress-up?

Absolutely! It brings out a very safe way to communicate even deeper fantasies. Whether the costume is sensual or humorous, it becomes a vehicle of expression, a way to say and show what you want without exposing yourself, so to speak. And, it can make you feel sexy, sinister, nasty, whorish, sweet, innocent, trashy … all in one week. Cool!

How can fetish gear play a role?

Adding a real stethoscope to the doctor outfit? Helloooooo. Oh, and those clamps! Wow. I'm getting hot just thinking about it. Fetish gear offers a higher level of realism, which intensifies the fantasy and the result. The gear is also "converted" to serve sexual purposes for very naughty, nasty, fun, and cool turn-ons.

What's the key to making a memorable threesome?

Participating with unabashed lust and passion. Let go. Everything else will come.

PLAYING THE GAME

Putting on the clothes that correspond with the role you're playing can make it easier to stay in character and really imagine what it's like to be someone else during your sexual play. It's hard not to get into the moment when you're wearing the right outfit! It's also easier to let go of inhibitions if you're someone else.

THINGS TO KEEP IN MIND

If you're renting a costume, make sure you don't get too carried away with it and rip it; you'll have to pay for it if you do. Alternately, make sure you have it cleaned before you return it. If you own the costume, you have fewer worries depending on how particular you are about ensuring its pristine appearance. The main thing to keep in mind? Let go and have fun with it!

> It's totally different when you are one of two women than when you are the girl with two men. I think everyone should try both.
> —PATRICIA LEE, EROSBOUTIQUE.COM

LOCATION CHANGES

Once you've done all you can possibly do in the confines of your own home, it's time to test out what you can do elsewhere! Sometimes a change of venue is all you need to make everything seem new again, and sometimes a change of venue can provide new inspiration for sexual adventures!

ALTERNATE HOMES

If you always have your threesome at your place, why not have it at your significant other's place for a change, or even at your third's home? You never know what kind of new and inventive things you can find to work with in a new setting, be it a different room or an inspiring piece of furniture. Just the opportunity to see another side of the people you're having sex with can be enough to change your perspective on things or show you something you didn't know before!

HOTELS

If something about threesoming in your home just doesn't feel right anymore, a hotel is a fantastic alternative and one that can ramp up role-playing or dress-up fantasies. For example, the tone you can set by attempting a threesome at a divey roadside motel is different from what you get renting out the penthouse suite at a luxury hotel. Both are equally fun, it's all just a matter of what works for your pocketbook. Also, getting a hotel room can sometimes help shed inhibitions because it will feel like you're on vacation from your normal life. And who doesn't feel freer on vacation?

GETAWAYS

Who says you can't take your threesome on the road? Maybe the three of you can take a camping trip and devise clever ways to stay warm when the sun goes down, or the three of you decide to hop a plane to the ultimate adult playground, Las Vegas. No matter what the destination, changing cities can really change your view of what is and isn't possible in your threesome.

ODD SPOTS

Don't count out places you've never thought of for a little fun! For example, you can always have a romp in the car—it's challenging, but it's possible! If your balcony is private (or even if it isn't, depending on how daring you want to be) why not move the party out there? Hallways, kitchens, anyplace that doesn't have a bed is fair game. The best odd spot to take your threesome? The bathroom—especially if you have a tub that fits all three of you! What better way to get clean and dirty at the same time.

INDOOR VS. OUTDOOR, PUBLIC VS. PRIVATE

For the truly adventurous outdoor sex might be the jolt you're looking for. But be careful! Just because the three of you are into public sex doesn't mean everyone else will be. Have public sex in the wrong spot and you could run the risk of arrest!

That said, sometimes the thrill of potentially getting caught is half the fun! Try semi-secluded areas in parks, elevators, movie theaters— even creative manipulations on airplanes can be done! Are you really into putting on a show? Maybe it's time to hit that swingers' party or sex club as a threesome and really turn some heads!

QUICKIES VS. LONG, DRAWN-OUT AFFAIRS

Another way to change up the pace of your threesome is to literally change the pace. Do you always take your time in your threesome, exploring every inch of each of your lovers' bodies over and over? Do you get in a quick and dirty where you can? Well maybe it's time to try the other side of things.

THE JOY OF QUICKIES

One thing is for certain. In the sexual lexicon, the quickie should not be discounted as less pleasing than its more drawn-out counterparts. What if the three of you are at a party and can't escape until after a certain time? A quickie in the bathroom is a great way to tide you over until you can really get down to business, not to mention whet your whistle for later! Besides, if you know just the right buttons to press during that quickie, and find creative ways to press them throughout the night, you can keep your partners' motors running all night long.

Three ... In Literature

Deeming itself as American as Adam, Eve, and apple pie, *Three in Love* aimed to detail ménages à trois from ancient to modern times while discussing the intricacies of threesomes, proclaiming them the Next Big Thing in relationships. The book does discuss much of the history and theory behind the whos and whys of threesomes but the most interesting part about it is that it's written by a threesome engaged in a relationship, Barbara and Michael Foster with Letha Hadday. This provides living proof that three isn't always a crowd. Featuring discussions about the lifestyle, the beauty of the experience and stories of lives in triad, *Three in Love* helps show that threesomes are as valid as other relationship in life.

After spending an evening at a party telling each other what we were going to do to one another, the walk home became a little too much for me, my boyfriend, and a girlfriend of mine to stand. We were all so turned on from all the hot talk we'd been engaging in—and in public, no less!—that we ducked into an alleyway on the walk home and started to go at it right then and there. Sure, it wasn't the most romantic of spots— we were right next to a Dumpster that smelled really foul, but the urgency of the situation and the fact that we were out there in the open made us forget about everything else and concentrate on each other. Hot doesn't even begin to describe it! —BEATRICE R., 33

THE JOY OF LONG, DRAWN-OUT AFFAIRS

On the flip side of things, having an endless sex session can be pure bliss. If you've gone for what feels like hours and you still don't feel completely fulfilled, why not make one full day a sex day with your partners? Turn it into a marathon session where anything goes from sun up until sun down. You and yours will be guaranteed to finish the day with a permanent smile on your face!

By this point you've definitely had your fun, but do you know how to properly draw things to a close? Well, you're about to find out!

Once we spent an entire day naked, just the three of us. And, of course, spending the day naked meant we couldn't resist playing all day. Sometimes two of us would be sitting on the couch watching TV, and someone else would join us and step up the game. Or I'd be in the bathtub, and they'd come in and help make sure I was extra clean. Making dinner that night was definitely an event. By the time we were done, there was more food on us than on our plates, so we spent a lot of time making sure every last bit was eaten! It was quite a treat. —PETER J., 34

three to go

If getting your

threesome started is the first point of
anxiety, how to end it is a close second.
When all is said and done, when and
how do you make your bow?
When you've reached the final moments
of your experience, realizing you've
expended the maximum amount of
sexual energy you're going to put forth
for that day, take a moment to revel in
what you've just done. After all, it's an
accomplishment!

DRAWING THINGS TO A CLOSE

When all is said and done, there are right and wrong ways to leave your sexual bliss (or non-bliss, as the case may be). Even if your experience didn't turn out to be what you'd hoped and dreamed it would, that's no excuse to leave things badly. There are two other people to consider, after all.

WHEN YOU'RE ALL DONE

When you were in the planning stages of your threesome, chances are you and yours already had a discussion of whether or not sleeping over was appropriate. If not, now's the time to have that discussion in a very lighthearted way.

IF YOU'RE DONE AND THEY'RE NOT

There's always the possibility that you've had enough, but the other two are still rarin' to go. If you're comfortable with letting them play without you, there's no harm in telling them to go to town while you catch up on some much-needed rest. And who's to say that you won't be ready to go again after a quick little catnap?

If you're not comfortable with them playing without you, respectfully request that the fun draw to a close for now, and suggest (if you had a good time) that you revisit it at a later date. As with all the other games you've been playing, your partners should respect your decision and respond accordingly.

IF THEY'RE DONE AND YOU'RE NOT

Unfortunately, you're out of luck on this one. Just like if you were done and they weren't, you're going to have to respect when your partners say they're finished. If nothing else, pat yourself on the back. You wore them out! And again, a catnap can do wonders. You never know what you might be able to start up again after everyone has had a little r n' r.

Three ... In Film

Sunday Bloody Sunday was a groundbreaking film, being the first widely distributed major motion picture to depict two men in bed, but that's not the whole story. Following a threesome relationship between a homosexual man (Murray Head), heterosexual woman (Glenda Jackson), and bisexual man (Peter Finch), *Sunday Bloody Sunday* tells of how a young woman and a doctor discover they're sharing the same man, and make the decision to keep sharing him for fear of losing him. Directed by John Schlesinger, the movie was nominated for four Academy Awards and won the BAFTA Award for Best Film.

The second it was over we were all exhausted. It was like the culmination of everything we'd been working toward for so long just drained us of every ounce of our energy. We didn't really have a talk about whether or not someone should sleep over, but by that point it didn't matter. We were all so wiped out that we just fell asleep in each other's arms. It was very peaceful, and felt really natural. —NATALIE S., 23

SPENDING THE NIGHT

To some it might seem like spending the night after a sexual encounter is a no-brainer, while to others it might seem like the last thing in the world they would want to do. Everyone has a preference, but when it comes to threesomes, figuring out if all three meet on the same page can be a little complicated.

SHOULD YOU SPEND THE NIGHT?

If you're not having your threesome on your own turf, think ahead and decide whether or not you want to spend the night ahead of time. Though you might go into the experience knowing for certain that you don't, it's possible that after all is said and done that you might want to sleep over after all. Of course, there's the possibility that you're not welcome to, in which case, no matter how put out you feel, you have to respect your host's wishes.

SHOULD THEY SPEND THE NIGHT?

If the threesome is taking place at your home and sleeping arrangements haven't been discussed, it's something you might want to think about. If you don't mind someone sleeping over but don't want them to share your bed, there's nothing wrong with setting them up in a spare room or on the couch with a pillow and blankets. There's also the possibility that they don't want to sleep over. In that case, don't take it personally.

HOW TO POLITELY DECLINE A SLEEPOVER

If you're a third—or a couple—having a threesome at a location other than your own home and you're invited to spend the night but don't want to, there's no reason to be nasty about it. If it's just not something with which you feel comfortable, just be up front and tell

Spending the night can strengthen your bond as three.

them it's not something you feel ready for. However, do make sure that they know you're grateful for the experience you just shared.

If you're a third—or a couple—having a threesome at your own home and you don't want someone to spend the night, it's best to make that clear from the outset so there aren't any awkward moments when the event has drawn to a close. That way everyone knows that when it's done, *it's done* and they're prepared for departure. If you change your mind in the middle of the action and figure a sleepover isn't something you really want to do, tell your partners you're worn out and need some peace and quiet to recharge your batteries. If they don't understand, you might not be having a threesome with the right people.

The first time I had a threesome, I didn't think I was ever going to sleep. I was running on all cylinders all night, to the point where my girlfriend thought I had Energizer batteries inside! When she and our third pooped out, I let them sleep for a while to regain their strength, and then teasingly woke them both up for another round. There was something really fun about sexually rousing them from their sleep that they requested we do it like that every time! —WARREN P., 25

DOING A WRAP-UP WITH YOUR PARTNER

Just like a coach sits down with his team after a game to discuss the win or loss, you'll want to sit down with your partner after your threesome and do a wrap-up. What was good, what—if anything—was bad, and what would you like to do again?

WHERE AND WHEN
Your post-threesome wrap-up can take place almost anywhere: at home, over dinner, on a lovely walk outdoors. Choose a place that makes you two feel peaceful and comfortable. That means no discussions in a noisy bar. You're just not going to get anything done that way.

An Expert Opinion:

Writer and Sexpert Emily Dubberley on "how to end your threesome the right way"

Making a good first impression is important, but it's often the way we say goodbye that leaves the most lasting impression. Emily Dubberley, founder of cliterati.co.uk and author of Brief Encounters: The Women's Guide to Casual Sex, *shares her thoughts on how to properly and gracefully end a highly sexual evening, especially if you want to do it again.*

Have you ever had a threesome?

I never talk about my own sex life but I certainly know a lot of people who've had group sex in every iteration and am well aware of the pros and cons!

What are your top etiquette tips for successful threesomes?

Set the guidelines, stick to them, practice safer sex, say if you feel uncomfortable at any stage, and make sure everyone's on the same page. Although it can be easier for it to happen when drunk, it's better to get informed consent from everyone when sober as otherwise things can go pear-shaped.

How should you close things down when the action is done?

Go to sleep and have a civilized breakfast in the morning, unless it's been particularly traumatic, in which case getting a cab home is a better bet.

What if things are awkward afterward, be it the morning after, or even weeks later?

The best thing is to be honest about your feelings. If you're with a partner and you feel insecure about the relationship afterward, tell your partner and arrange a special date to remind each other that you are still a strong couple. If it was with a friend and the friendship has suffered, talk through why you feel strange. It may be that only time will heal, but it's worth facing any problems as soon as possible so they don't fester.

Is it rude to get up and go when everything is done?

If you feel uncomfortable at any stage it's fine to leave. Just make sure the other people know it's not their fault (unless it is!). Chances are, they'll understand. Threesomes don't suit everyone and something that seems fun in fantasy may be scary or less desirable in reality.

What are your tips for dealing with the aftermath if it's traumatic?

Be honest to yourself and the other people concerned. If you're really traumatized, get counseling. And don't do it again!

How long should people wait to try another one if it's been traumatic?

It depends on why it was traumatic. If it was because of the other people concerned, don't have another threeway with them. If it was because of your own behavior, look at the reasons you acted as you did and, should the opportunity arise again, make sure you don't repeat your mistakes. You certainly shouldn't feel obliged to have a threesome again if you didn't enjoy it the first time. At the same time, threesomes are as different as relationships. Just because this one didn't work doesn't mean another one wouldn't.

What if the threesome was at your place and you want them to leave when you're done? How do you address it?

Ideally address it beforehand by saying that you have a friend/family member coming around in the morning so they can't stay. If you haven't addressed it before, get out of bed afterward, put your clothes on and make coffee in another room, then invite the other people to have coffee with you in that room. Getting them out of your bed or wherever the threesome location is the easiest way to then get them out the door.

Is it customary for people to spend the night, or is it okay to ask them to leave?

If someone's good enough to have sex with, they should be good enough to share your bed for a night—though, unless you have a huge bed, you may

find it more comfortable if you all huddle up under a duvet on the floor. That's obviously assuming that things have gone well.

Do you recommend doing a post-threesome wrap-up with your partner?

I wouldn't recommend threesomes with a partner. I think it's better with friends or strangers (as long as you're safe). I've seen too many relationships fall apart because of threesomes. But yes, if you do have a threesome with a partner you should definitely talk about it before and after. After a threesome, talk to your partner about how it made you feel. Mention any insecurities it brought up for you (if any) and ask if they have any so that you can make them feel better. Make a point of pampering your partner. Arrange a special date for the pair of you the next day to normalize things for you as a couple. Some couples enjoy talking dirty about the threesome as sex play after the event, but it's important to make sure they're not feeling insecure before plunging into talk about how hot the experience was.

How should you leave things when all is said and done if you want to do it again? Or if you don't want to do it again?

Exchange numbers or not. The etiquette is the same as with normal dating, in my opinion. Be honest, communicate what you want and don't be selfish. All too often in threesomes, one person will get ignored, so make sure that doesn't happen. And afterward, don't take someone's number if you don't want to see them again. There's no point leading someone on.

How can you ensure it will become a repeat event?

You can't, but being polite, sticking to guidelines, showing your enjoyment, and making it clear you'd be up for it again (without sounding desperate) are all a good start. Say thanks very much, that was fun, or something similar. You can do this verbally, send a text, or leave a voice message after the event. Don't make more than one call, though. The other people may not have the same attitude as you do. You'll want to give them a chance to respond.

When depends on how both you and your partner feel in the aftermath of your threesome. Once again, use your instincts. If by the next morning your partner seems cheery and okay with the situation, you could address it right then and there over breakfast. If he or she seems withdrawn and contemplative, you might want to allow them some time to sort through some feelings. And if he or she is angry, ask why, and make sure it's clear you want to discuss it when they're ready. However, be prepared to wait. Your partner may need a chance to calm down.

WHAT TO DISCUSS

First off, ask your partner how they felt about the experience. Was it good or bad? Did it meet expectations, fail to, or exceed them? What were the best parts of it? Was there anything bad about it? If you were to do anything differently the next time, what would it be? Will there be a next time?

One thing to keep in mind while you're talking with your partner is that you don't want to judge him or her. You might think something that happened wasn't that great, while your lover thinks it was the greatest thing ever. On the flipside, you might have enjoyed the experience much more than he or she did, which might raise an issue: If you enjoyed it to the point where you want to do it again, and you're alone in that, what next? You may have to make a decision about whether or not you should give up your partner or the fantasy of another threesome.

You'll want to keep the lines of communication open, making it comfortable and safe for both you and your partner to voice your opinions about what went down. Sometimes that's the most valuable step to ensuring the event will happen again (if that's what you want).

Have one-on-one time with your partner when all is said and done.

Three ... In Film

Many people point to *Splash* as Darryl Hannah's hottest movie, and while it rates right up there, 1982's *Summer Lovers* put her in a completely different position, and it sizzled. Shot in Santorini, Greece, Hannah plays the girlfriend of Peter Gallagher. The two take a romantic trip to Greece, where Gallagher falls for a French archaeologist working on a dig, played by Valerie Quennessen. When Hannah goes to confront her over the affair, the two women find themselves drawn to one another, which sets up the threesome relationship. The result is a beautiful and sexual film that takes an alternate look at threesome relationships—namely, that they can be achieved in perfect harmony.

IF YOU WANT TO DO IT AGAIN

If your threesome was a good enough time that you know you want to give it another shot, there's nothing wrong with sharing that sentiment with your partner. One of the ways you can express it most effectively is if you say how good an experience it was to share with each other, which should reinforce the security you'd need to move forward with another threesome. By the same token, be open to the fact that your partner may have to do a little more processing before feeling ready to give it another go. Don't push anything. Just as when you were first planning your threesome, getting too aggressive is a surefire way to ensure it'll never happen again—with that partner, anyway.

IF YOU DON'T WANT TO DO IT AGAIN

As with anything, honesty is always the best policy. Tell your partner what it was you didn't like about the experience, and why it was enough to convince you a threesome isn't something you want to try again. Or, maybe the event was so good that you feel the one experience was enough to satiate you, and you're ready to move on to other things. If your partner is adamant that it happen again despite your wishes otherwise, you might have to reconsider this person as a part of your life. But, it's likely if you had the communication skills to lead you to a threesome in the first place, your lover will respect your wishes and feelings about the situation.

Three... In Television

You wouldn't think that threesomes would have a place in sci-fi shows, but you'd be wrong. Three characters on *Battlestar Galactica* did exactly that with explosive results. After a series of complicated events, a threesome begins between Dr. Gaius Baltar (James Callis) and the humanoid cylons Number Three (Lucy Lawless) and Number Six (Tricia Helfer). What started as a coupling between Baltar and Six turned into a threesome when Three mistook Baltar's nonsensical ramblings during a torture session as love for her, when he was actually hallucinating that he was talking to Six. As the threesome picks up steam, Six confesses that she's in love with both Baltar and Three, which is something Three and Baltar echo, until the two of them break up with Six several episodes later, claiming they have different destinies. Though it ends in tragedy, the threesome between Three, Six, and Baltar is the hottest storyline the series has ever seen, and gave many a sci-fi fan fantasy material for decades to come.

HOW TO MAKE SURE IT HAPPENS AGAIN

Though nothing in life is a guarantee, there are certainly steps to take to encourage a repeat of your threesome. First off, if the discussion with your partner goes well, you know you're in the clear. But the question is whether you want to have a threesome with the same people or someone new?

TRYING WITH THE SAME PEOPLE

If you and your partner want to have a threesome with the same person, make sure to also do a follow up with your third to see how he or she felt about the experience. If you hear that all was well and they enjoyed it just as much as you did, then all systems are go! You can always suggest the three of you hang out together sometime and see where it leads from there, or if you're more of the planning type, set a date with all involved.

TRYING WITH DIFFERENT PEOPLE

If your third isn't into the idea of giving it another go, just go back to the first chapter and look at some of your other options. Maybe you and your partner can seek out someone new, be it by using an online dating site, trying a sex club, or seeing who in your social circle might be an appropriate replacement for your last partner. And don't take it personally, because it might not be about you. If your third tells you it's because of something you did, try to rectify the situation and mend the relationship, or at least end things on a positive note.

DESPERATION PROS AND CONS

Different people will have different attitudes about whether or not begging and pleading for another shot is hot or not, and you probably know with which person you're threesoming. There's nothing wrong with a little playful cajoling if that's the kind of relationship you have, but if not, constantly bringing it up and pleading for it will just serve to create a rift between you and yours, and irritate all involved. It's best to steer clear of the desperate act just to be on the safe side.

It took a little while for me to work up the courage to discuss everything with my girlfriend. I think I was afraid she didn't like it. The funny thing was, she was afraid of the same thing, but when we compared notes we realized it was such an amazing event that we wanted it to happen again and again. I think having threesomes has actually helped us grow stronger as a couple, physically, mentally, and spiritually. The connection we share with each other stemming from the sexual experiences we have as a couple is just incredible. —ALEX F., 33

So there you have it.

Your complete guide to achieving, executing, and sustaining threesome sex. Of course, like anything in life, you have to take these tips and make them your own in an effort to make the experience something that's truly and uniquely you. If you've read this far, chances are that you're either well on your way to making that happen, or you've already made it happen again and again. Regardless of which category you fall into, remember: It's your sex life to do with as you choose. Variety is the spice of life, and threesomes can be a really great compliment to an already tasty dish.

Index